MY SPECIAL GIFT TO YOU...

Congratulations on having taken the first step toward abundance and prosperity! As a special "thank you" for picking up Richest Man In Babylon Decoded, I'd like to offer you 2 special bonuses that will really help you take advantage of the lessons you're about to learn in this book.

1. Affirmations for Affluence

A companion to the chapter "Seven Cures For A Lean Purse," these affirmations will embed powerful new beliefs and behaviors into your subconscious, and help you attain a mind focused on limitless opportunities for wealth. This is the secret to getting the kind of abundant life that you deserve.

2. Insider Money Saving Tips

These invaluable tips will help you save thousands of dollars a year on necessities if done right. You're getting advice straight from today's best financial experts, at absolutely no cost at all. Save big on your car, entertainment, grocery, and home maintenance, so you can look forward to a fatter bank account for your retirement needs, or even if you need a little extra cash to treat yourself every year with a well deserved holiday.

To your abundant wealth,

Winter Vee

Winter Vee

CLAIM YOUR BONUSES
WORTH $197 HERE:

www.RichestManDecoded.com/bonus

RICHEST MAN IN

BABYLON DECODED

By George Samuel Clason

Compiled And Edited By Winter Vee

RICHEST MAN IN BABYLON DECODED

Contents

Contents

Contents

Contents

TO THE READER

Dear Friend,

If you have ever struggled with obtaining or retaining wealth, then picking up this book is probably the best decision you have ever made in your life.

Many who have read The Richest Man In Babylon have found themselves inspired by the tales of personal wealth within its pages.

Considered to be one of the top best-selling motivational books, this timeless classic comes highly recommended by the world's most successful executives, managers, and entrepreneurs who have blazed a trail of success using the wisdoms found in George Clason's original text.

I remember picking up The Richest Man In Babylon when I was at the absolute lowest point in my life. My businesses had left me in debt to the IRS to the tune of over $32,000, which forced me to take a low paying job that I soon lost... on my 26th birthday, no less.

Being unemployed afforded me the time to really look at myself and my life. As I wandered through the local mall, it was by sheer chance that I came upon The Richest Man In Babylon in a bookstore.

I got the book because I was desperate to turn my life around any way I could.

As cliché as this sounds, it changed my life forever. The Richest Man In Babylon changed everything I knew about obtaining and retaining wealth, and gave me a deep understanding of why most people (including myself at the time) consistently fail to manifest, or even hold onto any semblance of wealth in their lives.

Once I applied the lessons as I understood them, I was able to not only get myself out of debt, but I was also able to attract and take advantage of many wealth generating opportunities that allowed me to live the kind of life that I had always wanted for myself.

I now have the freedom to travel the world and work when I want, where I want, because of everything I've learned from The Richest Man In Babylon.

It is my goal to help you understand all of Clason's wisdoms, which is why I've written this book, The Richest Man In Babylon Decoded.

The book you hold in your hand contains wisdoms from a bygone era, wisdoms that still apply to this day. Because Clason's original text was published back in 1926, some of the language used may seem somewhat archaic, and a little difficult to understand for some people.

Therefore, I have distilled and "decoded" - hence the title of the book - the wisdoms that Clason has tried to impart unto us with his original text.

I have retained Clason's timeless classic in its entirety, however you will find that at the end of every chapter, I have added brief Summaries that explain succinctly Clason's original text.

I have included all new modern day interpretations of the timeless stories as told by Clason, in the hopes that it makes it easier for you, the reader, to better understand The Richest Man In Babylon.

If you don't feel like reading through every word of Clason's original text and just want to get right to the good stuff, then you may refer to the Summaries to get a quick overview of what each chapter is about.

But more importantly, after each Summary, you'll find Learning Lessons featuring personal insights and case studies relevant to the lessons that each chapter conveys.

I have also included some practical strategies that you may want to try and apply to your life.

To benefit fully from this book, I highly advise that you TAKE ACTION, by applying the lessons and strategies that you will learn in this book.

Remember, change only happens when you take action.

If you want to live the kind of life where wealth comes abundantly, where you never have to worry about paying next month's rent, or even never having to think twice about buying something that catches your eye as it sits on display in a store window...

Then you have to take action once you have obtained the knowledge necessary to enact change in your life.

Without further ado, let's step through the mists of time and into ancient Babylon, where wisdom awaits.

Winter Vee

Winter Vee

ABOUT THE AUTHORS

GEORGE SAMUEL CLASON

George Samuel Clason was born in Louisiana, Missouri, on November 7, 1874. He attended the University of Nebraska and served in the United States Army during the Spanish-American War.

Beginning a long career in publishing, he founded the Clason Map Company of Denver, Colorado, and published the first road atlas of the United States and Canada. In 1926, he issued the first of a famous series of pamphlets on thrift and financial success, using parables set in ancient Babylon to make each of his points.

These were distributed in large quantities by banks and insurance companies and became familiar to millions, the most famous being "The Richest Man in Babylon," the parable from which the present volume takes its title. These "Babylonian parables" have become a modern inspirational classic.

ABOUT THE AUTHORS

WINTER VEE

Winter has always been an entrepreneur at heart. Dropping out of high school at age 17, he took his GED and began working. He didn't find high school engaging - both academically and socially - having taught himself HTML at the age of 11.

As a young man, he found himself working for other businesses, including well-known large corporations. This was counter to what he saw growing-up as both of his parents were entrepreneurs.

After being laid off at his last place of business (2 days after his 26th birthday and 2 days before Christmas) he decided to become a freelance network engineer, before trying out a friend's line of online, entrepreneur work, which opened the door to a whole new, and yet familiar life.

Despite a myriad of personal struggles, Winter has used the laws of manifestation to build a 7-figure business, and in the last 2 years, has been able to maintain 4 residences in different cities, 4 automobiles, and travel the world at his leisure - all while maintaining and building a multi-million dollar business.

FOREWORD

Our prosperity as a nation depends upon the personal financial prosperity of each of us as individuals.

This book deals with the personal successes of each of us. Success means accomplishments as the result of our own efforts and abilities. Proper preparation is the key to our success. Our acts can be no wiser than our thoughts. Our thinking can be no wiser than our understanding.

This book of cures for lean purses has been termed a guide to financial understanding. That, indeed, is its purpose: to offer those who are ambitious for financial success an insight which will aid them to acquire money, to keep money and to make their surpluses earn more money.

In the pages which follow, we are taken back to Babylon, the cradle in which was nurtured the basic principles of finance now recognized and used the world over.

To new readers the author is happy to extend the wish that its pages may contain for them the same inspiration for growing bank accounts, greater financial successes and the solution of difficult personal financial problems so enthusiastically reported by readers from coast to coast.

To the business executives who have distributed these tales in such generous quantities to friends, relatives, employees and associates, the author takes this opportunity to express his gratitude.

No endorsement could be higher than that of practical men who appreciate its teachings because they, themselves, have worked up to important successes by applying the very principles it advocates.

Babylon became the wealthiest city of the ancient world because its citizens were the richest people of their time. They appreciated the value of money. They practiced sound financial principles in acquiring money, keeping money and making their money earn more money. They provided for themselves what we all desire...incomes for the future.

G. S. C.

AN HISTORICAL SKETCH OF BABYLON.

In the pages of history there lives no city more glamorous than Babylon. Its very name conjures visions of wealth and splendor. Its treasures of gold and jewels were fabulous. One naturally pictures such a wealthy city as located in a suitable setting of tropical luxury, surrounded by rich natural resources of forests, and mines.

Such was not the case. It was located beside the Euphrates River, in a flat, arid valley. It had no forests, no mines—not even stone for building. It was not even located upon a natural trade-route. The rainfall was insufficient to raise crops.

Babylon is an outstanding example of man's ability to achieve great objectives, using whatever means are at his disposal. All of the resources supporting this large city were man-developed. All of its riches were man-made.

Babylon possessed just two natural resources—a fertile soil and water in the river. With one of the greatest engineering accomplishments of this or any other day, Babylonian engineers diverted the waters from the river by means of dams and immense irrigation canals.

Far out across that arid valley went these canals to pour the life giving waters over the fertile soil. This ranks among the first engineering feats known to history. Such abundant crops as were the reward of this irrigation system the world had never seen before.

Fortunately, during its long existence, Babylon was ruled by successive lines of kings to whom conquest and plunder were but incidental. While it engaged in many wars, most of these were local or defensive against ambitious conquerors from other countries who coveted the fabulous treasures of Babylon.

The outstanding rulers of Babylon live in history because of their wisdom, enterprise and justice. Babylon produced no strutting monarchs who sought to conquer the known world that all nations might pay homage to their egotism.

As a city, Babylon exists no more. When those energizing human forces that built and maintained the city for thousands of years were withdrawn, it soon became a deserted ruin. The site of the city is in Asia about six hundred miles east of the Suez Canal, just north of the Persian Gulf. The latitude is about thirty degrees above the Equator, practically the same as that of Yuma, Arizona. It possessed a climate similar to that of this American city, hot and dry.

Today, this valley of the Euphrates, once a populous irrigated farming district, is again a wind-swept arid waste. Scant grass and desert shrubs strive for existence against the windblown sands. Gone are the fertile fields, the mammoth cities and the long caravans of rich merchandise. Nomadic bands of Arabs, securing a scant living by tending small herds, are the only inhabitants. Such it has been since about the beginning of the Christian era.

Dotting this valley are earthen hills. For centuries, they were considered by travelers to be nothing else. The attention of archaeologists were finally attracted to them because of broken pieces of pottery and brick washed down by the occasional rain storms. Expeditions, financed by European and American museums, were sent here to excavate and see what could be found. Picks and shovels soon proved these hills to be ancient cities. City graves, they might well be called.

Babylon was one of these. Over it for something like twenty centuries, the winds had scattered the desert dust. Built originally of brick, all exposed walls had disintegrated and gone back to earth once more.

Such is Babylon, the wealthy city, today. A heap of dirt, so long abandoned that no living person even knew its name until it was discovered by carefully removing the refuse of centuries from the streets and the fallen wreckage of its noble temples and palaces.

Many scientists consider the civilization of Babylon and other cities in this valley to be the oldest of which there is a definite record. Positive dates have been proved reaching back 8000 years.

An interesting fact in this connection is the means used to determine these dates. Uncovered in the ruins of Babylon were descriptions of an eclipse of the sun. Modern astronomers readily computed the time when such an eclipse, visible in Babylon, occurred and thus established a known relationship between their calendar and our own.

In this way, we have proved that 8000 years ago, the Sumerites, who inhabited Babylonia, were living in walled cities. One can only conjecture for how many centuries previous such cities had existed. Their inhabitants were not mere barbarians living within protecting walls.

They were an educated and enlightened people. So far as written history goes, they were the first engineers, the first astronomers, the first mathematicians, the first financiers and the first people to have a written language.

Mention has already been made of the irrigation systems which transformed the arid valley into an agricultural paradise. The remains of these canals can still be traced, although they are mostly filled with accumulated sand.

Some of them were of such size that, when empty of water, a dozen horses could be ridden abreast along their bottoms. In size they compare favorably with the largest canals in Colorado and Utah.

In addition to irrigating the valley lands, Babylonian engineers completed another project of similar magnitude. By means of an elaborate drainage system they reclaimed an immense area of swamp land at the mouths of the Euphrates and Tigris Rivers and put this also under cultivation.

Herodotus, the Greek traveler and historian, visited Babylon while it was in its prime and has given us the only known description by an outsider. His writings give a graphic description of the city and some of the unusual customs of its people. He mentions the remarkable fertility of the soil and the bountiful harvest of wheat and barley which they produced.

The glory of Babylon has faded but its wisdom has been preserved for us. For this we are indebted to their form of records. In that distant day, the use of paper had not been invented. Instead, they laboriously engraved their writing upon tablets of moist clay. When completed, these were baked and became hard tile. In size, they were about six by eight inches, and an inch in thickness.

These clay tablets, as they are commonly called, were used much as we use modern forms of writing. Upon them were engraved legends, poetry, history, transcriptions of royal decrees, the laws of the land, titles to property, promissory notes and even letters which were dispatched by messengers to distant cities.

From these clay tablets we are permitted an insight into the intimate, personal affairs of the people. For example, one tablet, evidently from the records of a country storekeeper, relates that upon the given date a certain named customer brought in a cow and exchanged it for seven sacks of wheat, three being delivered at the time and the other four to await the customer's pleasure.

Safely buried in the wrecked cities, archaeologists have recovered entire libraries of these tablets, hundreds of thousands of them.

One of the outstanding wonders of Babylon was the immense walls surrounding the city. The ancients ranked them with the great pyramid of Egypt as belonging to the "seven wonders of the world." Queen Semiramis is credited with having erected the first walls during the early history of the city.

Modern excavators have been unable to find any trace of the original walls. Nor is their exact height known. From mention made by early writers, it is estimated they were about fifty to sixty feet high, faced on the outer side with burnt brick and further protected by a deep moat of water.

The later and more famous walls were started about six hundred years before the time of Christ by King Nabopolassar. Upon such a gigantic scale did he plan the rebuilding, he did not live to see the work finished. This was left to his son, Nebuchadnezzar, whose name is familiar in Biblical history.

The height and length of these later walls staggers belief. They are reported upon reliable authority to have been about one hundred and sixty feet high, the equivalent of the height of a modern fifteen story office building. The total length is estimated as between nine and eleven miles.

So wide was the top that a six-horse chariot could be driven around them. Of this tremendous structure, little now remains except portions of the foundations and the moat. In addition to the ravages of the elements, the Arabs completed the destruction by quarrying the brick for building purposes elsewhere.

Against the walls of Babylon marched, in turn, the victorious armies of almost every conqueror of that age of wars of conquest. A host of kings laid siege to Babylon, but always in vain. Invading armies of that day were not to be considered lightly.

Historians speak of such units as 10,000 horsemen, 25,000 chariots, 1200 regiments of foot soldiers with 1000 men to the regiment. Often two or three years of preparation would be required to assemble war materials and depots of food along the proposed line of march. The city of Babylon was organized much like a modern city. There were streets and shops.

Peddlers offered their wares through residential districts. Priests officiated in magnificent temples.

Within the city was an inner enclosure for the royal palaces. The walls about this were said to have been higher than those about the city.

The Babylonians were skilled in the arts. These included sculpture, painting, weaving, gold working and the manufacture of metal weapons and agricultural implements. Their Jewellers created most artistic jewellery. Many samples have been recovered from the graves of its wealthy citizens and are now on exhibition in the leading museums of the world.

At a very early period when the rest of the world was still hacking at trees with stone-headed axes, or hunting and fighting with flint-pointed spears and arrows, the Babylonians were using axes, spears and arrows with metal heads.

The Babylonians were clever financiers and traders. So far as we know, they were the original inventors of money as a means of exchange, of promissory notes and written titles to property.

Babylon was never entered by hostile armies until about 540 years before the birth of Christ.

Even then the walls were not captured. The story of the fall of Babylon is most unusual. Cyrus, one of the great conquerors of that period, intended to attack the city and hoped to take its impregnable walls.

Advisors of Nabonidus, the King of Babylon, persuaded him to go forth to meet Cyrus and give him battle without waiting for the city to be besieged. In the succeeding defeat to the Babylonian army, it fled away from the city. Cyrus, thereupon, entered the open gates and took possession without resistance.

Thereafter the power and prestige of the city gradually waned until, in the course of a few hundred years, it was eventually abandoned, deserted, left for the winds and storms to level once again to that desert earth from which its grandeur had originally been built. Babylon had fallen, never to rise again, but to it civilization owes much.

The eons of time have crumbled to dust the proud walls of its temples, but the wisdom of Babylon endures.

Money is the medium by which earthly success is measured.

Money makes possible the enjoyment of the best the earth affords.

Money is plentiful for those who understand the simple laws which govern its acquisition.

Money is governed today by the same laws which controlled it when prosperous men thronged the streets of Babylon, six thousand years ago.

THE MAN WHO DESIRED GOLD

Bansir, the chariot builder of Babylon, was thoroughly discouraged. From his seat upon the low wall surrounding his property, he gazed sadly at his simple home and the open workshop in which stood a partially completed chariot.

His wife frequently appeared at the open door. Her furtive glances in his direction reminded him that the meal bag was almost empty and he should be at work finishing the chariot, hammering and hewing, polishing and painting, stretching taut the leather over the wheel rims, preparing it for delivery so he could collect from his wealthy customer.

Nevertheless, his fat, muscular body sat stolidly upon the wall. His slow mind was struggling patiently with a problem for which he could find no answer.

The hot, tropical sun, so typical of this valley of the Euphrates, beat down upon him mercilessly. Beads of perspiration formed upon his brow and trickled down unnoticed to lose themselves in tie hairy jungle on his chest.

Beyond his home towered the high terraced wall surrounding the king's palace. Nearby, cleaving the blue heavens, was the painted tower of the Temple of Bel. In the shadow of such grandeur was his simple home and many others far less neat and well cared for. Babylon was like this — a mixture of grandeur and squalor, of dazzling wealth and direst poverty, crowded together without plan or system within the protecting walls of the city.

Behind him, had he cared to turn and look, the noisy chariots of the rich jostled and crowded aside the sandaled tradesmen as well as the barefooted beggars.

Even the rich were forced to turn into the gutters to clear the way for the long lines of slave water carriers, on the "King's Business," each bearing a heavy goatskin of water to be poured upon the hanging gardens.

Bansir was too engrossed in his own problem to hear or heed the confused hubbub of the busy city. It was the unexpected twanging of the strings from a familiar lyre that aroused him from his reverie. He turned and looked into the sensitive, smiling face of his best friend — Kobbi, the musician.

"May the Gods bless thee with great liberality, my good friend," began Kobbi with an elaborate salute. "Yet, it does appear they have already been so generous thou needest not to labor. I rejoice with thee in thy good fortune. More, I would even share it with thee. Pray, from thy purse which must be bulging else thou wouldst be busy in your shop, extract but two humble shekels and lend them to me until after the noblemen's feast this night. Thou wilt not miss them ere they are returned."

"If I did have two shekels," Bansir responded gloomily, "to no one could I lend them — not even to you, my best of friends; for they would be my fortune — my entire fortune. No one lends his entire fortune, not even to his best friend."

"What," exclaimed Kobbi with genuine surprise, "Thou hast not one shekel in thy purse, yet sit like a statue upon a wall! Why not complete that chariot? How else canst thou provide for thy noble appetite? Tis not like thee, my friend. Where is thy endless energy? Doth something distress thee? Have the Gods brought to thee troubles?"

"A torment from the Gods it must be," Bansir agreed. "It began with a dream, a senseless dream, in which I thought I was a man of means. From my belt hung a handsome purse, heavy with coins.

There were shekels which I cast with careless freedom to the beggars; there were pieces of silver with which I did buy finery for my wife and whatever I did desire for myself; there were pieces of gold which made me feel assured of the future and unafraid to spend the silver. A glorious feeling of contentment was within me! You would not have known me for thy hardworking friend. Nor wouldst have known my wife, so free from wrinkles was her face and shining with happiness. She was again the smiling maiden of our early married days."

"A pleasant dream, indeed," commented Kobbi, "but why should such pleasant feelings as it aroused turn thee into a glum statue upon the wall?"

"Why, indeed! Because when I awoke and remembered how empty was my purse, a feeling of rebellion swept over me. Let us talk it over together, for, as the sailors do say, we ride in the same boat, we two. As youngsters, we went together to the priests to learn wisdom. As young men, we shared each other's pleasures.

As grown men, we have always been close friends. We have been contented subjects of our kind. We have been satisfied to work long hours and spend our earnings freely. We have earned much coin in the years that have passed, yet to know the joys that come from wealth, we must dream about them. Bah! Are we more than dumb sheep? We live in the richest city in all the world. The travelers do say none equals it in wealth.

About us is much display of wealth, but of it we ourselves have naught. After half a lifetime of hard labor, thou, my best of friends, hast an empty purse and sayest to me, "May I borrow such a trifle as two shekels until after the noblemen's feast this night?" Then, what do I reply? Do I say, "Here is my purse; its contents will I gladly share?'

No, I admit that my purse is as empty as thine. What is the matter? Why cannot we acquire silver and gold — more than enough for food and robes?

"Consider, also, our sons," Bansir continued, "are they not 17following in the footsteps of their fathers? Need they and their families and their sons and their sons' families live all their lives in the midst of such treasurers of gold, and yet, like us, be content to banquet upon sour goat's milk and porridge?"

"Never, in all the years of our friendship, didst thou talk like this before, Bansir." Kobbi was puzzled.

"Never in all those years did I think like this before. From early dawn until darkness stopped me, I have labored to build the finest chariots any man could make, soft- heartedly hoping some day the Gods would recognize my worthy deeds and bestow upon me great prosperity.

This they have never done. At last, I realize this they will never do. Therefore, my heart is sad. I wish to be a man of means. I wish to own lands and cattle, to have fine robes and coins in my purse. I am willing to work for these things with all the strength in my back, with all the skill in my hands, with all the cunning in my mind, but I wish my labors to be fairly rewarded. What is the matter with us?

Again I ask you! Why cannot we have our just share of the good things so plentiful for those who have the gold with which to buy them?"

"Would I knew an answer!" Kobbi replied. "No better than thou am I satisfied.

My earnings from my lyre are quickly gone. Often must I plan and scheme that my family be not hungry.

Also, within my breast is a deep longing for a lyre large enough that it may truly sing the strains of music that do surge through my mind. With such an instrument could I make music finer than even the king has heard before."

"Such a lyre thou shouldst have. No man in all Babylon could make it sing more sweetly; could make it sing so sweetly, not only the king but the Gods themselves would be delighted. But how mayest thou secure it while we both of us are as poor as the king's slaves? Listen to the bell! Here they come."

He pointed to the long column of half naked, sweating water bearers plodding laboriously up the narrow street from the river. Five abreast they marched, each bent under a heavy goatskin of water.

"A fine figure of a man, he who doth lead them." Kobbi indicated the wearer of the bell who marched in front without a load. "A prominent man in his own country, 'tis easy to see."

"There are many good figures in the line," Bansir agreed, "as good men as we. Tall, blond men from the north, laughing black men from the south, little brown men from the nearer countries. All marching together from the river to the gardens, back and forth, day after day, year after year. Naught of happiness to look forward to. Beds of straw upon which to sleep — hard grain porridge to eat. Pity the poor brutes, Kobbi!"

"Pity them I do. Yet, thou dost make me see how little better off are we, free men though we call ourselves."

That is truth, Kobbi, unpleasant thought though it be. We do not wish to go on year after year living slavish lives. Working, working, working! Getting nowhere."

"Might we not find out how others acquire gold and do as they do?" Kobbi inquired.

"Perhaps there is some secret we might learn if we but sought from those who knew," replied Bansir thoughtfully.

"This very day," suggested Kobbi, "I did pass our old friend, Arkad, riding in his golden chariot. This I will say, he did not look over my humble head as many in his station might consider his right. Instead, he did wave his hand that all onlookers might see him pay greetings and bestow his smile of friendship upon Kobbi, the musician."

"He is claimed to be the richest man in all Babylon," Bansir mused.

"So rich the king is said to seek his golden aid in affairs of the treasury," Kobbi replied. "So rich," Bansir interrupted, "I fear if I should meet him in the darkness of the night, I should lay my hands upon his fat wallet."

"Nonsense," reproved Kobbi, "a man's wealth is not in the purse he carries. A fat purse quickly empties if there be no golden stream to refill it. Arkad has an income that constantly keeps his purse full, no matter how liberally he spends."

"Income, that is the thing," ejaculated Bansir. "I wish an income that will keep flowing into my purse whether I sit upon the wall or travel to far lands. Arkad must know how a man can make an income for himself. Dost suppose it is something he could make clear to a mind as slow as mine?"

"Methinks he did teach his knowledge to his son, Nomasir," Kobbi responded.

"Did he not go to Nineveh and, so it is told at the inn, become, without aid from his father, one of the richest men in that city?"

"Kobbi, thou bringest to me a rare thought." A new light gleamed in Bansir's eyes. "It costs nothing to ask wise advice from a good friend and Arkad was always that. Never mind though our purses be as empty as the falcon's nest of a year ago. Let that not detain us. We are weary of being without gold in the midst of plenty.

We wish to become men of means. Come, let us go to Arkad and ask how we, also, may acquire incomes for ourselves."

Thou speakest with true inspiration, Bansir. Thou bringeth to my mind a new understanding.

Thou makest me to realize the reason why we have never found any measure of wealth. We never sought it. Thou hast labored patiently to build the staunchest chariots in Babylon. To that purpose was devoted your best endeavors. Therefore, at it thou didst succeed. I strove to become a skillful lyre player. And, at it I did succeed.

"In those things toward which we exerted our best endeavors we succeeded.

The Gods were content to let us continue thus. Now, at last, we see a light, bright like that from the rising sun. It biddeth us to learn more that we may prosper more. With a new understanding we shall find honourable ways to accomplish our desires."

"Let us go to Arkad this very day," Bansir urged, "Also, let us ask other friends of our boyhood days, who have fared no better than ourselves, to join us that they, too, may share in his wisdom."

"Thou wert ever thus thoughtful of thy friends, Bansir. Therefore hast thou many friends. It shall be as thou sayest. We go this day and take them with us."

SUMMARY
Guide

Bansir was a man who built chariots. However he was dissatisfied with his lot in life because of a recent dream - a dream in which he was flaunting wealth and happy and contented.

He confided in his friend Kobbi the musician the epiphany he had - Why was he not wealthy at all, especially when others were? Why could he not earn more? Why could he not have more? Where was all the gold?

The pair then reminisced about their youth, and how they were earning a decent living all this while, and yet, at this point in time they had nothing to show for it and still slogging away for their livelihood.

As the two mused about their situation, the topic came to their common friend Arkad, who was proclaimed as the richest man in Babylon. The pair decided that they would pay a visit to Arkad and find out how he got it right and came to be in the envious position that he was now, living the life of rich and wealth.

Perhaps there was some secret they could emulate?

If you look closely, the pair hit upon the answer they needed earlier in their conversation:

"Arkad has an income that constantly keeps his purse full, no matter how liberally he spends."

The key word - Income.

In this modern day, how can a person live comfortably, like how Arkad did? By having a passive income.

Say, for example, you step out into society to work. You start earning money. You start spending money.

Among the things you need to set aside money for - Food, rent, transport, insurance, allowance for the parents, study loans, etc.

Then you might start dating, maybe get married... so you will also have to provide for your own family.

As time goes by, you keep earnin, but you also keep spending. The money, the wealth goes in and out.

However, if you have some form of passive income coming in, and if you also actively build it up and top up your own earnings, this technically means that you are never poor and struggling!

Towards the end of the chapter, Kobbi hit the nail on the head regarding the underlying factor for their "failures":

"Thou makest me to realize the reason why we have never found any measure of wealth. We never sought it."

Above all, it is Bansir, and Kobbi, who never sought wealth.

If you think of it, if you don't seek it, wealth will never line itself in your purse or wallet.

Just as like attracts like, people never become wealthy because they never directed their mind, or actions, to actively pursuing it.

It all boils down to the simple, first step of a mindset built for wealth:

You must visualize wealth in order to welcome wealth.

You have to do it on a regular basis, every day; there's no excuse or 'but' about it.

In the following visualization technique that will kick-start your journey to wealth, you will be specifically using as many of your 5 senses as you can.

Why?

Because since forever, humans have used all 5 senses to explore the world and make sense of it. It is these 5 senses that makes us so vested in our existence, and thus it makes sense to use all of them in our visualization strategy.

Here's how you take the first step to manifesting your deserved wealth and abundance in your life:

🏛 **Step 1**: Find a place where you can carry out the visualization exercise in relative peace and minimal distractions. If possible, switch off your cellphone or to set it to silent.

🏛 **Step 2**: Next, come up with a figure or amount that you would like to see yourself earn by the end of the year. This amount should be something realistic and not overly improbable.

🏛 **Step 3**: Have a comfortable seat. If possible, wear loose clothing so that you are not restricted in any way. Be mindful of proper posture; don't slouch.

🏛 **Step 4**: Set a timer for the visualization exercise. It can be 5 or 10 minutes, or according to your preference.

🏛 **Step 5**: Close your eyes, practice smooth breathing and start visualizing with your 5 senses. See and visualize the amount in your mind. Feel the dollar bills with your fingers.

Smell the crisp fragrance of the notes. Hear the bank note-counting machine going through that wealth. Taste the indulgent foods you've longed to experience. Use your imagination. Keep these coming in and feel it strongly in your mind.

Visualize also what you're doing to do with that wealth. A luxurious family vacation? A swanky new ride? An upscale district deluxe pad rivaling that of Hollywood stars'?

🏛 **Step 6**: As the timer starts counting down, allow yourself to return to the present, slowly but surely.

Do this visualization exercise 2 - 3 times a day. It is all right if you are unable to sustain the visualization for your timing in the beginning. Work at it and strengthen yourself gradually.

That being said, the results of your visualization may manifest in other forms and not necessarily money itself. So, do open your eyes and see the opportunities being presented to you.

THE RICHEST MAN IN BABYLON

In old Babylon there once lived a certain very rich man named Arkad. Far and wide he was famed for his great wealth. Also was be famed for his liberality. He was generous in his charities. He was generous with his family. He was liberal in his own expenses. But nevertheless each year his wealth increased more rapidly than he spent it.

And there were certain friends of younger days who came to him and said: "You, Arkad, are more fortunate than we. You have become the richest man in all Babylon while we struggle for existence. You can wear the finest garments and you can enjoy the rarest foods, while we must be content if we can clothe our families in raiment that is presentable and feed them as best we can.

"Yet, once we were equal. We studied under the same master. We played in the same games. And in neither the studies nor the games did you outshine us. And in the years since, you have been no more an honorable citizen than we.

"Nor have you worked harder or more faithfully, insofar as we can judge. Why, then, should a fickle fate single you out to enjoy all the good things of life and ignore us who are equally deserving?"

Thereupon Arkad remonstrated with them, saying, "If you have not acquired more than a bare existence in the years since we were youths, it is because you either have failed to learn the laws that govern the building of wealth, or else you do not observe them.

"Fickle Fate' is a vicious goddess who brings no permanent good to anyone. On the contrary, she brings ruin to almost every man upon whom she showers unearned gold. She makes wanton spenders, who soon dissipate all they receive and are left beset by overwhelming appetites and desires they have not the ability to gratify.

Yet others whom she favors become misers and hoard their wealth, fearing to spend what they have, knowing they do not possess the ability to replace it. They further are beset by fear of robbers and doom themselves to lives of emptiness and secret misery.

"Others there probably are, who can take unearned gold and add to it and continue to be happy and contented citizens. But so few are they, I know of them but by hearsay. Think you of the men who have inherited sudden wealth, and see if these things are not so.

"His friends admitted that of the men they knew who had inherited wealth these words were true, and they besought him to explain to them how he had become possessed of so much prosperity, so he continued: "In my youth I looked about me and saw all the good things there were to bring happiness and contentment. And I realized that wealth increased the potency of all these. "Wealth is a power. With wealth many things are possible.

"One may ornament the home with the richest of furnishings. "One may sail the distant seas.

"One may feast on the delicacies of far lands.

"One may buy the ornaments of the gold worker and the stone polisher.

"One may even build mighty temples for the Gods.

"One may do all these things and many others in which there is delight for the senses and gratification for the soul.

"And, when I realized all this, I decided to myself that I would claim my share of the good things of life. I would not be one of those who stand afar off, enviously watching others enjoy. I would not be content to clothe myself in the cheapest raiment that looked respectable.

I would not be satisfied with the lot of a poor man. On the contrary, I would make myself a guest at this banquet of good things.

"Being, as you know, the son of a humble merchant, one of a large family with no hope of an inheritance, and not being endowed, as you have so frankly said, with superior powers or wisdom, I decided that if I was to achieve what I desired, time and study would be required.

"As for time, all men have it in abundance. You, each of you, have let slip by sufficient time to have made yourselves wealthy. Yet, you admit; you have nothing to show except your good families, of which you can be justly proud.

"As for study, did not our wise teacher teach us that learning was of two kinds: the one kind being the things we learned and knew, and the other being the training that taught us how to find out what we did not know?

"Therefore did I decide to find out how one might accumulate wealth, and when I had found out, to make this my task and do it well. For, is it not wise that we should enjoy while we dwell in the brightness of the sunshine, for sorrows enough shall descend upon us when we depart for the darkness of the world of spirit?

"I found employment as a scribe in the hall of records, and long hours each day I labored upon the clay tablets. Week after week, and month after month, I labored, yet for my 24earnings I had naught to show.

Food and clothing and penance to the gods, and other things of which I could remember not what, absorbed all my earnings. But my determination did not leave me.

"And one day Algamish, the money lender, came to the house of the city master and ordered a copy of the Ninth Law, and he said to me, I must have this in two days, and if the task is done by that time, two coppers will I give to thee."

"So I labored hard, but the law was long, and when Algamish returned the task was unfinished.

He was angry, and had I been his slave, he would have beaten me. But knowing the city master would not permit him to injure me, I was unafraid, so I said to him, 'Algamish, you are a very rich man. Tell me how I may also become rich, and all night I will carve upon the clay, and when the sun rises it shall be completed.'

"He smiled at me and replied, 'You are a forward knave, but we will call it a bargain.'

"All that night I carved, though my back pained and the smell of the wick made my head ache until my eyes could hardly see. But when he returned at sunup, the tablets were complete.

"Now,' I said, 'tell me what you promised.'

"You have fulfilled your part of our bargain, my son,' he said to me kindly, 'and I am ready to fulfill mine. I will tell you these things you wish to know because I am becoming an old man, and an old tongue loves to wag. And when youth comes to age for advice he receives the wisdom of years.

But too often does youth think that age knows only the wisdom of days that are gone, and therefore profits not. But remember this, the sun that shines today is the sun that shone when thy father was born, and will still be shining when thy last grandchild shall pass into the darkness.

"The thoughts of youth,' he continued, 'are bright lights that shine forth like the meteors that oft make brilliant the sky, but the wisdom of age is like the fixed stars that shine so unchanged that the sailor may depend upon them to steer his course.

"Mark you well my words, for if you do not you will fail to grasp the truth that I will tell you, and you will think that your night's work has been in vain.'

"Then he looked at me shrewdly from under his shaggy brows and said in a low, forceful tone,

'I found the road to wealth when I decided that a part of all I earned was mine to keep. And so will you.'

"Then he continued to look at me with a glance that I could feel pierce me but said no more.

"Is that all?' I asked.

"That was sufficient to change the heart of a sheep herder into the heart of a money lender,' he replied.

"But all I earn is mine to keep, is it not?' I demanded.

"Far from it,' he replied. 'Do you not pay the garment- maker? Do you not pay the sandal-maker? Do you not pay for the things you eat? Can you live in Babylon without spending?

What have you to show for your earnings of the past mouth? What for the past year? Fool! You pay to everyone but yourself. Dullard, you labor for others. As well be a slave and work for what your master gives you to eat and wear. If you did keep for yourself one-tenth of all you earn, how much would you have in ten years?'

"My knowledge of the numbers did not forsake me, and I answered, 'As much as I earn in one year.'

"You speak but half the truth,' he retorted. 'Every gold piece you save is a slave to work for you. Every copper it earns is its child that also can earn for you. If you would become wealthy, then what you save must earn, and its children must earn, that all may help to give to you the abundance you crave.

"You think I cheat you for your long night's work,' he continued, 'but I am paying you a thousand times over if you have the intelligence to grasp the truth I offer you.

"A part of all you earn is yours to keep. It should be not less than a tenth no matter how little you earn. It can be as much more as you can afford. Pay yourself first. Do not buy from the clothes-maker and the sandal-maker more than you can pay out of the rest and still have enough for food and charity and penance to the gods.

"Wealth, like a tree, grows from a tiny seed. The first copper you save is the seed from which your tree of wealth shall grow. The sooner you plant that seed the sooner shall the tree grow. And the more faithfully you nourish and water that tree with consistent savings, the sooner may you bask in contentment beneath its shade.'

"So saying, he took his tablets and went away.

"I thought much about what he had said to me, and it seemed reasonable. So I decided that I would try it. Each time I was paid I took one from each ten pieces of copper and hid it away. And strange as it may seem, I was no shorter of funds, than before. I noticed little difference as I managed to get along without it. But often I was tempted, as my hoard began to grow, to spend it for some of the good things the merchants displayed, brought by camels and ships from the land of the Phoenicians. But I wisely refrained.

"A twelfth month after Algamish had gone he again returned and said to me, 'Son, have you paid to yourself not less than one-tenth of all you have earned for the past year?'

"I answered proudly, 'Yes, master, I have.' 'That is good,' he answered beaming upon me, 'and what have you done with it?"

"I have given it to Azmur, the brick maker, who told me he was traveling over the far seas and in Tyre he would buy for me the rare jewels of the Phoenicians. When he returns we shall sell these at high prices and divide the earnings."

"Every fool must learn," he growled, 'but why trust the knowledge of a brick maker about jewels? Would you go to the bread maker to inquire about the stars? No, by my tunic, you would go to the astrologer, if you had power to think. Your savings are gone, youth, you have jerked your wealth-tree up by the roots. But plant another.

Try again. And next time if you would have advice about jewels, go to the jewel merchant. If you would know the truth about sheep, go to the herdsman. Advice is one thing that is freely given away, but watch that you take only what is worth having. He who takes advice about his savings from one who is inexperienced in such matters, shall pay with his savings for proving the falsity of their opinions." Saying this, he went away.

"And It was as he said. For the Phoenicians are scoundrels and sold to Azmur worthless bits of glass that looked like gems. But as Algamish had bid me, I again saved each tenth copper, for I now had formed the habit and it was no longer difficult.

"Again, twelve months later, Algamish came to the room of the scribes and addressed me.

"What progress have you made since last I saw you?"

"I have paid myself faithfully,' I replied, 'and my savings I have entrusted to Agger the shield maker, to buy bronze, and each fourth month he does pay me the rental."

"That is good. And what do you do with the rental?' "I do have a great feast with honey and fine wine and spiced cake. Also I have bought me a scarlet tunic. And some day I shall buy me a young ass upon which to ride." To which Algamish laughed, "You do eat the children of your savings. Then how do you expect them to work for you?

And how can they have children that will also work for you?

First get thee an army of golden slaves and then many a rich banquet may you enjoy without regret." So saying he again went away.

"Nor did I again see him for two years, when he once more returned and his face was full of deep lines and his eyes drooped, for he was becoming a very old man. And he said to me, "Arkad, hast thou yet achieved the wealth thou dreamed of?"

And I answered, "Not yet all that I desire, but some I have and it earns more, and its earnings earn more."

"And do you still take the advice of brick makers?"

"About brick making they give good advice," I retorted.

"Arkad," he continued, "you have learned your lessons well. You first learned to live upon less than you could earn. Next you learned to seek advice from those who were competent through their own experiences to give it. And, lastly, you have learned to make gold work for you."

"You have taught yourself how to acquire money, how to keep it, and how to use it. Therefore, you are competent for a responsible position.

I am becoming an old man. My sons think only of spending and give no thought to earning. My interests are great and I fear too much for me to look after. If you will go to Nippur and look after my lands there, I shall make you my partner and you shall share in my estate."

"So I went to Nippur and took charge of his holdings, which were large. And because I was full of ambition and because I had mastered the three laws of successfully handling wealth, I was enabled to increase greatly the value of his properties.

So I prospered much, and when the spirit of Algamish departed for the sphere of darkness, I did share in his estate as he had arranged under the law." So spake Arkad, and when he had finished his tale, one of his friends said, "You were indeed fortunate that Algamish made of you an heir."

"Fortunate only in that I had the desire to prosper before I first met him. For four years did I not prove my definiteness of purpose by keeping one-tenth of all earned? Would you call a fisherman lucky who for years so studied the habits of the fish that with each changing wind he could cast his nets about them? Opportunity is a haughty goddess who wastes no time with those who are unprepared."

"You had strong will power to keep on after you lost your first year's savings. You are unusual in that way," spoke up another.

"Will power!" retorted Arkad. "What nonsense. Do you think will power gives a man the strength to lift a burden the camel cannot carry, or to draw a load the oxen cannot budge? Will power is but the unflinching purpose to carry a task you set for yourself to fulfillment. If I set for myself a task, be it ever so trifling, I shall see it through.

How else shall I have confidence in myself to do important things? Should I say to myself, 'For a hundred days as I walk across the bridge into the city, I will pick from the road a pebble and cast it into the stream,' I would do it.

If on the seventh day I passed by without remembering, I would not say to myself, Tomorrow I will cast two pebbles which will do as well.' Instead, I would retrace my steps and cast the pebble. Nor on the twentieth day would I say to myself, 'Arkad, this is useless. What does it avail you to cast a pebble every day? Throw in a handful and be done with it.' No, I would not say that nor do it. When I set a task for myself, I complete it.

Therefore, I am careful not to start difficult and impractical tasks, because I love leisure."

And then another friend spoke up and said, "If what you tell is true, and it does seem as you have said, reasonable, then being so simple, if all men did it, there would not be enough wealth to go around."

Wealth grows wherever men exert energy," Arkad replied. "If a rich man builds him a new palace, is the gold he pays out gone? No, the brickmaker has part of it and the laborer has part of it, and the artist has part of it. And everyone who labors upon the house has part of it.

Yet when the palace is completed, is it not worth all it cost? And is the ground upon which it stands not worth more because it is there? And is the ground that adjoins it not worth more because it is there? Wealth grows in magic ways. No man can prophesy the limit of it. Have not the Phoenicians built great cities on barren coasts with the wealth that comes from their ships of commerce on the seas?"

"What then do you advise us to do that we also may become rich?" asked still another of his friends. "The years have passed and we are no longer young men and we have nothing put by."

"I advise that you take the wisdom of Algamish and say to yourselves, 'A part of all I earn is mine to keep.' Say it in the morning when you first arise. Say it at noon. Say it at night. Say it each hour of every day. Say it to yourself until the words stand out like letters of fire across the sky.

"Impress yourself with the idea. Fill yourself with the thought. Then take whatever portion seems wise. Let it be not less than one-tenth and lay it by. Arrange your other expenditures to do this if necessary. But lay by that portion first. Soon you will realize what a rich feeling it is to own a treasure upon which you alone have claim. As it grows it will stimulate you. A new joy of life will thrill you.

Greater efforts will come to you to earn more. For of your increased earnings, will not the same percentage be also yours to keep?

"Then learn to make your treasure work for you. Make it your slave. Make its children and its children's children work for you.

"Insure an income for thy future. Look thou at the aged and forget not that in the days to come thou also will be numbered among them. Therefore invest thy treasure with greatest caution that it be not lost. Usurious rates of return are deceitful sirens that sing but to lure the unwary upon the rocks of loss and remorse.

"Provide also that thy family may not want should the Gods call thee to their realms. For such protection it is always possible to make provision with small payments at regular intervals. Therefore the provident man delays not in expectation of a large sum becoming available for such a wise purpose.

"Counsel with wise men. Seek the advice of men whose daily work is handling money. Let them save you from such an error as I myself made in entrusting my money to the judgment of Azmur, the brickmaker. A small return and a safe one is far more desirable than risk.

"Enjoy life while you are here. Do not overstrain or try to save too much. If one-tenth of all you earn is as much as you can comfortably keep, be content to keep this portion. Live otherwise according to your income and let not yourself get niggardly and afraid to spend. Life is good and life is rich with things worthwhile and things to enjoy."

His friends thanked him and went away. Some were silent because they had no imagination and could not understand. Some were sarcastic because they thought that one so rich should divide with old friends not so fortunate. But some had in their eyes a new light.

They realized that Algamish had come back each time to the room of the scribes because he was watching a man work his way out of darkness into light. When that man had found the light, a place awaited him. No one could fill that place until he had for himself worked out his own understanding, until he was ready for opportunity.

These latter were the ones, who, in the following years, frequently revisited Arkad, who received them gladly. He counseled with them and gave them freely of his wisdom as men of broad experience are always glad to do. And he assisted them in so investing their savings that it would bring in a good interest with safety and would neither be lost nor entangled in investments that paid no dividends.

The turning point in these men's lives came upon that day when they realized the truth that had come from Algamish to Arkad and from Arkad to them.

A Part Of All You Earn Is Yours To Keep

SUMMARY Guide

The viewpoint now moves to Arkad. Because of his success, his childhood friends came up to him, curious about the mechanism of his success, because the wealth disparity between him and them were too great!

Arkad then related his own experience:

He used to labor day and night as a scribe, week after week, month after month. However he still had nothing to show for it.

One day, a moneylender Algamish turned up to use his scribing services, but Arkad was unable to produce the results. Instead he asked Algamish to teach him how to become wealthy. In exchange he promised he would complete the job by hook or by crook.

So, he worked day and night on the scribing tablet and finally completed it. Algamish kept his word and explained that one was to keep a part of all he earned. It should not be less than a tenth, no matter the amount earned. However the amount he saved he gave it to Azmur the brick maker who bought back worthless jewels and he could not sell them.

Algamish told Arkad to start saving again. When Algamish turned up 12 months later, Arkad explained that he loaned it to a bronze maker to purchase bronze, and who paid him back rental every 4 months.

With that gold, Arkad spent it. Algamish admonished him and advised him to use to use the gold to work for him instead. 2 years later, Algamish returned once again. While Arkad did not make it big, he learned to use the advice of the brick maker to his advantage.

Algamish invited Arkad to Nippur to look after his lands and be a working partner. Subsequently Arkad was able to increase the value of Algamish's properties. Eventually Algamish passed away and left his lands to Arkad and that how he made it rich.

At this point, Arkad finished his story, and his friends now knew how he came by his wealth. To them, he advised: First, take a part of all one earned to keep. Second, make those savings work. Thirdly, learn to invest with the greatest caution. Lastly, learn to enjoy life too.

LEARNING/LESSON

In this chapter, we have a few learning lessons, so let's go through them one by one.

#1: "A part of all you earn is yours to keep. It should be not less than a tenth no matter how little you earn. It can be as much more as you can afford. Pay yourself first ."

Essentially, this is very clear cut.

Of whatever you earn, keep aside one tenth - in other words, 10% - consistently. Make it a habit.

If you have too many essential commitments (debts, study loan etc) that exceeds 90% of what you can spend, this means you have less than 10% to save. What happens then?

In such a case, you can play around with the numbers. Maybe start by saving 5%. You can gradually increase it to 10% once you've cleared your essential commitments.

The point is to start saving.

What happens when you do that? It means that you spend only 90% of your paycheck instead of 100%. Is that a lot?
Does it affect your current quality of life?

Actually, no.

It may make you tweak your current expenses a little, but that's it. Basically, it doesn't - and shouldn't - compromise your standard of living. You definitely can still enjoy your luxury moments, but there are surely some items you can live without.

Eventually you'll see that the material things you used to splurge on, hey, they don't matter so much anymore. Yes, you still enjoy and pamper yourself, but the 10% you put aside will do more for you than you can ever imagine!

So, don't hesitate, start saving the 10% now! Saving money is the easiest of all:

🏛 **Step 1**: Withdraw the money (10% of the total paycheck) when it is deposited into your account, or count it out when you receive it in cash.

🏛 **Step 2**: Save it in a savings jar or a bank account (separate from your usual bank account for expenditure purposes), and watch it GROW.

#2: "Advice is one thing that is freely given away, but watch that you take only what is worth having. He who takes advice about his savings from one who is inexperienced in such matters, shall pay with his savings for proving the falsity of their opinions."

What happened when Algamish returned for the first time?

Arkad revealed that he passed his savings to a brick maker, to buy back jewels. If you look at it, what do bricks have anything to do with jewels?

And how was Arkad rewarded with his investment? Worthless jewels.

Arkad learnt his lesson; he invested his next sum of savings with Agger the shield maker to make his bronze shields. This investment is more sound because it taps on Agger's field of knowledge and specialty - bronze. And Arkad did earn his "commission" from his investment.

Therefore, it is prudent to invest wisely. If you do that, you will be rewarded with wealth, if not, you will lose it all, and have to start all over again.

To be honest, many self-proclaimed investors do not know their stuff. They may have made some good investments, and this misleads them into thinking that they are now masters of the trade. As such, others are taken in by their results and follow them blindly.

According to Forbes article, Why Smart People Fail To Beat The Market (Mar 12, 2012), there are only 2 ways to beat the stock market on a long term basis.

The first way is to possess superior knowledge. By this, it means you must have access to crucial information about the stock market and its inner workings. However it is widely known that fund managers and their analysts essentially under-perform.

Still, for those who made the cut, was it their skill or was it luck?
Yes, luck is the second way a person could theoretically beat the market. In A Random Walk Down Wall Street (1973), author Burton Malkiel wrote that "a blindfolded monkey throwing darts at a newspaper's financial pages could select a portfolio that would do just as well as one carefully selected by experts."

Essentially the premise is that luck would triumph as much over skill as possible.

In response to this, a Wall Street Journal Dartboard Contest emerged to test out Burton Malkiel's theory. The contest commenced in 1988, and over a hundred of them were completed at this time.

Each month, 4 leading Wall Street investment analysts were asked to pick one single stock that would perform the best. Next, 4 other stocks were randomly selected with the throw of the dart on the paper's stock pages. These stocks were printed for all to see. 6 months later, the stock results were tabulated.

It turned out that the experts clinched victory, however that was prior to risk adjustment. In addition, due to the public reporting of the stocks, a bias was created when people jumped to trade on those stocks the minute their identities were announced.

Therefore, in whatever investments you engage in, keep in mind that you're taking a risk. Do as much homework as you can.

Before you make an investment, consider these concerns:

- 🏛 What is your financial situation? Take a honest look at your entire financial well-being.

- 🏛 Evaluate your risk-taking aspect. Evaluate in 2 areas - your risk-taking capability and the risk of the investment category you're looking at.

- 🏛 Consider a diverse portfolio. By spreading out with different categories of investments (equity, bond, stock, cash, blue chips etc), this will significantly protect any dire losses.

- 🏛 Consider creating an emergency fund. This is also a protection measure, against heavy losses, or even, god forbid, bankruptcy. Some people put in at least 6 months' worth of savings.

#3: "You do eat the children of your savings. Then how do you expect them to work for you? And how can they have children that will also work for you? First get thee an army of golden slaves and then many a rich banquet may you enjoy without regret."

After Algamish came back the second time, he was aghast to learn that Arkad used the rental from the shield maker to indulge in a feast, bought some clothes and an animal for riding purposes.

The "children" essentially refers to the return, or the interest, on the initial amount of money, or the principal amount.

When there are returns on the principal amount, some people tend to be short-sighted and draw it out to spend, or that they may have some genuine cause to draw out the returns.

In investment wisdom, it is better to re-invest in the returns i.e. to make the "children" work for the benefits of the self.

Unless there is an overriding purpose to redeem the returns, continue re-investing it. Keep on growing the money tree. Look at the bigger picture, and learn to cultivate the patience to bring the investment to its culmination.

In order to look at the bigger picture, you can make your own money/wealth version of a vision board.

Generally, a vision board is a pictorial representation of your end-goals or dreams. For instance, for a person who dreams of getting fit, he or she usually goes through magazines or papers and cuts out pictures representing fitness (abs, muscles, slim and healthy built, exercise etc).

In this case:

🏛 **Step 1**: Get hold of a board, for a size of your preference.

🏛 **Step 2**: Get hold of magazines, especially wealth magazines (Money, Wealth, Forbes, Wall Street Journal etc), and cut out pictures which resonates THE MOST with you.

🏛 **Step 3**: Paste the pictures on the board and put up the board where you can see it on a every day basis, e.g. door of the room, or the home desk or fridge.

🏛 **Step 4**: Look at it for a few moments and visualize all those pictures coming true for you.

SEVEN CURES FOR A LEAN PURSE

The glory of Babylon endures. Down through the ages its reputation comes to us as the richest of cities, its treasures as fabulous.

Yet it was not always so. The riches of Babylon were the results of the wisdom of its people. They first had to learn how to become wealthy.

When the Good King, Sargon, returned to Babylon after defeating his enemies, the Elamites, he was confronted with a serious situation. The Royal Chancellor explained it to the King thus:

"After many years of great prosperity brought to our people because your majesty built the great irrigation canals and the mighty temples of the Gods, now that these works are completed the people seem unable to support themselves.

"The laborers are without employment. The merchants have few customers. The farmers are unable to sell their produce. The people have not enough gold to buy food."

"But where has all the gold gone that we spent for these great improvements?" demanded the King.

"It has found its way, I fear," responded the Chancellor, "into the possession of a few very rich men of our city.

It filtered through the fingers of most our people as quickly as the goat's milk goes through the strainer. Now that the stream of gold has ceased to flow, most of our people have nothing to for their earnings."

The King was thoughtful for some time. Then he asked, "Why should so few men be able to acquire all the gold?"

"Because they know how," replied the Chancellor. "One may not condemn a man for succeeding because he knows how. Neither may one with justice take away from a man what he has fairly earned, to give to men of less ability."

"But why," demanded the King, "should not all the people learn how to accumulate gold and therefore become themselves rich and prosperous?"

Quite possible, your excellency. But who can teach them? Certainly not the priests, because they know naught of money making."

"Who knows best in all our city how to become wealthy, Chancellor?" asked the King.

"Thy question answers itself, your majesty. Who has amassed the greatest wealth, in Babylon?"

"Well said, my able Chancellor. It is Arkad. He is richest man in Babylon. Bring him before me on the morrow."

Upon the following day, as the King had decreed, Arkad appeared before him, straight and sprightly despite his three score years and ten.

"Arkad," spoke the King, "is it true thou art the richest man in Babylon?"

"So it is reported, your majesty, and no man disputes it. "How becamest thou so wealthy?"

"By taking advantage of opportunities available to all citizens of our good city."

"Thou hadst nothing to start with?"

"Only a great desire for wealth. Besides this, nothing."

"Arkad," continued the King, "our city is in a very unhappy state because a few men know how to acquire wealth and therefore monopolize it, while the mass of our citizens lack the knowledge of how to keep any part of the gold they receive."

It is my desire that Babylon be the wealthiest city in the world. Therefore, it must be a city of many wealthy men. Therefore, we must teach all the people how to acquire riches. Tell me, Arkad, is there any secret to acquiring wealth? Can it be taught?"

"It is practical, your majesty. That which one man knows can be taught to others."

The king's eyes glowed. "Arkad, thou speaketh the words I wish to hear. Wilt thou lend thyself to this great cause? Wilt thou teach thy knowledge to a school for teachers, each of whom shall teach others until there are enough trained to teach these truths to every worthy subject in my domain?"

Arkad bowed and said, "I am thy humble servant to command. Whatever knowledge I possess will I gladly give for the betterment of my fellowmen and the glory of my King.

Let your good chancellor arrange for me a class of one hundred men and I will teach to them those seven cures which did fatten my purse, than which there was none leaner in all Babylon."

A fortnight later, in compliance with the King's command, the chosen hundred assembled in the great hall of the Temple of Learning, seated upon colorful rings in a semicircle.

Arkad sat beside a small taboret upon which smoked a sacred lamp sending forth a strange and pleasing odor.

"Behold the richest man in Babylon," whispered a student, nudging his neighbor as Arkad arose. "He is but a man even as the rest of us."

"As a dutiful subject of our great King," Arkad began, "I stand before you in his service.

Because once I was a poor youth who did greatly desire gold, and because I found knowledge that enabled me to acquire it, he asks that I impart unto you my knowledge.

"I started my fortune in the humblest way. I had no advantage not enjoyed as fully by you and every citizen in Babylon."

The first storehouse of my treasure was a well-purse. I loathed its useless emptiness. I desired it be round and full, clinking with the sound of gold. Therefore, I sought every remedy for a lean purse. I found seven.

"To you, who are assembled before me, shall I explain the seven cures for a lean purse which I do recommend to all men who desire much gold. Each day for seven days will I explain to you one of the seven remedies.

"Listen attentively to the knowledge that I will impart. Debate it with me. Discuss it among yourselves. Learn these lessons thoroughly, that ye may also plant in your own purse the seed of wealth.

First must each of you start wisely to build a fortune of his own. Then wilt thou be competent, and only then, to teach these truths to others.

"I shall teach to you in simple ways how to fatten your purses. This is the first step leading to the temple of wealth, and no man may climb who cannot plant his feet firmly upon the first step.

"We shall now consider the first cure."

THE FIRST CURE

START THY PURSE TO FATTENING.

Arkad addressed a thoughtful man in the second row. "My good friend, at what craft workest thou?"

"I," replied the man, "am a scribe and carve records upon the clay tablets."

"Even at such labor did I myself earn my first coppers. Therefore, thou hast the same opportunity to build a fortune."

He spoke to a florid-faced man, farther back. "Pray tell also what dost thou to earn thy bread?"

"I," responded this man, "am a meat butcher. I do buy the goats the farmers raise and kill them and sell the meat to the housewives and the hides to the sandal makers."

"Because thou dost also labor and earn, thou hast every advantage to succeed that I did possess."

In this way did Arkad proceed to find out how each man labored to earn his living. When he had done questioning them, he said:

"Now, my students, ye can see that there are many trades and labors at which men may earn coins.

Each of the ways of earning is a stream of gold from which the worker doth divert by his labors a portion to his own purse. Therefore into the purse of each of you flows a stream of coins large or small according to his ability. Is it not so?"

Thereupon they agreed that it was so. "Then," continued Arkad, "if each of you desireth to build for himself a fortune, is it not wise to start by utilizing that source of wealth which he already has established?"

To this they agreed.

Then Arkad turned to a humble man who had declared himself an egg merchant. "If thou select one of thy baskets and put into it each morning ten eggs and take out from it each evening nine eggs, what will eventually happen?"

"It will become in time overflowing."

"Why?"

"Because each day I put in one more egg than I take out."

Arkad turned to the class with a smile. "Does any man here have a lean purse?"

First they looked amused. Then they laughed. Lastly they waved their purses in jest.

"All right," he continued, "Now I shall tell thee the first remedy I learned to cure a lean purse.

Do exactly as I have suggested to the egg merchant. For every ten coins thou placest within thy purse take out for use but nine. Thy purse will start to fatten at once and its increasing weight will feel good in thy hand and bring satisfaction to thy soul.

"Deride not what I say because of its simplicity. Truth is always simple. I told thee I would tell how built my fortune.

This was my beginning. I, too, carried a lean purse and cursed it because there was naught within to satisfy my desires. But when I began to take out from my purse but nine parts of ten I put in, it began to fatten. So will thine.

"Now I will tell a strange truth, the reason for which I know not. When I ceased to pay out more than nine-tenths of my earnings, I managed to get along just as well. I was not shorter than before. Also, ere long, did coins come to me more easily than before. Surely it is a law of the Gods that unto him who keepeth and spendeth not a certain part of all his earnings, shall gold come more easily.

Likewise, him whose purse is empty does gold avoid.

"Which desirest thou the most? Is it the gratification of thy desires of each day, a jewel, a bit of finery, better raiment, more food; things quickly gone and forgotten? Or is it substantial belongings, gold, lands, herds, merchandise, income-bringing investments? The coins thou takest from thy purse bring the first. The coins thou leavest within it will bring the latter.

"This, my students, was the first cure I did discover for my lean purse: 'For each ten coins I put in, to spend but nine.' Debate this amongst yourselves. If any man proves it untrue, tell me upon the morrow when we shall meet again."

SUMMARY
Guide

After a victorious war over their enemies, the King of Babylon returned to the city. Upon his return, he was shocked to hear from his Chancellor that their citizens were now in dire straits. The current financial situation was such that a few people managed to amass unimaginable wealth while the population at large were now stricken with poverty.

Through his discussion with the Chancellor, the King decided to summon Arkad the richest man in Babylon to teach his people how to make themselves rich and prosperous, and to hold onto that wealth.

The following day, Arkad appeared before the King. The latter related the dismal state of affairs of the people to him, and Arkad agreed to teach a chosen hundred of his ways - the Seven Cures - to acquire, and sustain, wealth. This was to achieve an ambitious aim to make Babylon the wealthiest city in the world.

The chosen hundred gathered in the great hall of the Temple of Learning where Arkad explained his First Cure: Start thy purse to fattening.

Basically, each of them had a craft they practiced to bring in the income. Since the income is regular, it would be logical to start utilizing the recurring source of wealth.

His teaching was this: For every 10 coins which goes into the purse, take out 9 to use, and leave 1 within. The purse will start to fatten and eventually overflow.

LEARNING/LESSON

The underlying lesson for the First Cure is very simple: Spend less than you earn.

For every 10 dollars you earn, save 1 dollar.

If you recall, this is the same lesson as explored in the previous chapter, "The Richest Man In Babylon".

To re-cap,

🏛 **Step 1**: Withdraw the money (10% of the total paycheck) when it is deposited into your account, or count it out when you receive it in cash.

🏛 **Step 2**: Save it in a savings jar or a bank account (separate from your usual bank account for expenditure purposes), and watch it GROW.

For example, by saving 1 dollar, it means that only 9 dollars are not available for use, and somewhere along the line, we would need to tighten the spending.

Let's talk about the dollar you save.

If you're saving in a bank account, check out the competitive rates offered by the various banks. Some of them offer a sign-up bonus which you can take advantage of. Look at their interest rates as well and make an informed decision.

So, now with the savings you're implementing, you're left with 9 dollars to spend out of every 10 dollars. To some people, this would make a huge difference to their lifestyle, to others, not so much.

At this point in time, smart spending strategies need to be put into action. We came up with a few tips in the following categories:

🏛 **Car** - A clean air filter can improve gas mileage by 7%. This translates to about 100 dollars per 10,000 miles for an average car. Your manual should provide details on how to do that. If it is already in bad shape, consider changing it out; a new one goes for around 10 dollars or less at most stores.

🏛 **Electricity & Water** - Turn off the lights when you don't need them. If your home receives plenty of natural sunlight in the day, pull back the curtains and let it brighten up the house! Water that you use to wash vegetables or food can be used to water the plants.

🏛 **Entertainment** - Cut down on TV, be it the cable TV or Netflix. This will drastically reduce your cable bill. So what to do for entertainment?

One great way to fully make use of your time, meaningfully, is to volunteer. Whether it is at the retirement or nursing homes, or the orphanages or soup kitchens, there are many social causes that you can better put your time to.

At the end of the day, the experience is more fulfilling than you can ever imagine!

🏛 **Food** - Avoid convenience foods such as microwavable TV dinners or even fast food. Why? Simply because they are unhealthy. If you find yourself always hungry at work, keep healthy snacks in the break-room such as nuts, nutrient bars, digestive biscuits etc.

If you are able to cook, why not prepare 5 days worth of lunch over the weekend, freeze it, and then re-heat accordingly? This will likely take up only an hour or 2 of your day. In fact, create your meal plans by capitalizing on your local grocery store's flyer. You'll save money, and enjoy a lot of different meals!

🏛 **Reward & Membership** - Sign up with customer rewards program at the shops you patronize most often, especially the retailers where you get your groceries from. This will effectively help to save a lot of money. Do price comparisons if you can.

Look out for special discounts or discount coupons to make full use of them to stock up on non-perishables. For perishables, seek out the farmers' market where you can buy direct from the farmers without having to pay for transport, handling, storage fees if you had gotten them at the retailers.

THE SECOND CURE

CONTROL THY EXPENDITURES.

"Some of your members, my students, have asked me this: How can a man keep one-tenth of all he earns in his purse when all the coins he earns are not enough for his necessary expenses?" So did Arkad address his students upon the second day.

"Yesterday how many of thee carried lean purses?"

"All of us," answered the class.

"Yet, thou do not all earn the same. Some earn much more than others. Some have much larger families to support. Yet, all purses were equally lean. Now I will tell thee an unusual truth about men and sons of men. It is this; That what each of us calls our 'necessary expenses' will always grow to equal our incomes unless we protest to the contrary.

"Confuse not the necessary expenses with thy desires. Each of you, together with your good families, have more desires than your earnings can gratify. Therefore are thy earnings spent to gratify these desires insofar as they will go. Still thou retainest many ungratified desires.

"All men are burdened with more desires than they can gratify. Because of my wealth thinkest thou I may gratify every desire? 'Tis a false idea. There are limits to my time. There are limits to my strength. There are limits to the distance I may travel. There are limits to what I may eat. There are limits to the zest with which I may enjoy.

"I say to you that just as weeds grow in a field wherever the farmer leaves space for their roots, even so freely do desires grow in men whenever there is a possibility of their being gratified. Thy desires are a multitude and those that thou mayest gratify are but few.

"Study thoughtfully thy accustomed habits of living. Herein may be most often found certain accepted expenses that may wisely be reduced or eliminated. Let thy motto be one hundred percent of appreciated value demanded for each coin spent.

"Therefore, engrave upon the clay each thing for which thou desireth to spend. Select those that are necessary and others that are possible through the expenditure of nine- tenths of thy income. Cross out the rest and consider them but a part of that great multitude of desires that must go unsatisfied and regret them not.

"Budget then thy necessary expenses. Touch not the one- tenth that is fattening thy purse. Let this be thy great desire that is being fulfilled. Keep working with thy budget, keep adjusting it to help thee. Make it thy first assistant in defending thy fattening purse."

Hereupon one of the students, wearing a robe of red and gold, arose and said, "I am a free man.

I believe that it is my right to enjoy the good things of life. Therefore do I rebel against the slavery of a budget which determines just how much I may spend and for what. I feel it would take much pleasure from my life and make me little more than a pack-ass to carry a burden."

To him Arkad replied, "Who, my friend, would determine thy budget?"

"I would make it for myself," responded the protesting one.

"In that case were a pack-ass to budget his burden would he include therein jewels and rugs and heavy bars of gold? Not so. He would include hay and grain and a bag of water for the desert trail.

"The purpose of a budget is to help thy purse to fatten. It is to assist thee to have thy necessities and, insofar as attainable, thy other desires. It is to enable thee to realize thy most cherished desires by defending them from thy casual wishes. Like a bright light in a dark cave thy budget shows up the leaks from thy purse and enables thee to stop them and control thy expenditures for definite and gratifying purposes.

"This, then, is the second cure for a lean purse. Budget thy expenses that thou mayest have coins to pay for thy necessities, to pay for thy enjoyments and to gratify thy worthwhile desires without spending more than nine-tenths of thy earnings."

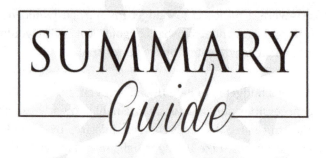

SUMMARY
Guide

The next day, Arkad imparted to the chosen hundred his second Cure: Control thy expenditures.

Be it men who earned more or men who earned less, they were all subjected to the same unusual truth: whatever was called "necessary expenses" would eventually grow to match the income.

He called upon them not to confuse necessary expenses with their own desires.

Men are burdened with more desires than they could ever gratify. Given the limited income, it would be impossible to satisfy each whim and fancy. Therefore it would be prudent to carefully examine the expenditures and the "necessary expenses" and reduce or eliminate accordingly.

In addition, the expenditures and the necessary expenses must only be fulfilled by the budget of 90% of the income. In other words, the 10% savings would remain in the purse.

LEARNING / LESSON

Compared to olden days, we have more desires to fulfill today, because we have grown to be a society fixated on consumerism, and whether we realize it or not, this fixation has become part of our every day psyche.

In the past, men's desire were on a par with their income, but now things have changed. Due to this simple concept of credit, our desire has grown way out of line.

Indeed, while it is human nature to desire for more, it is still equally possible to curb that human nature. So, to you, what defines as expenditure and what is the definition as a luxury expense?

Go through this quick quiz to gauge your understanding. Indicate with a check the category that the item belongs to: expenditure or luxury expense.

Item	Expenditure	Luxury
Accident insurance		
Backpacking trip fund		
Cab commute to work (too far)		
Car repayment		
Dining out		
Gym subscription		
Student loan		
The daily latte		
The new stereo set to play sleep-aiding music		

As you can see, some of the items may not look clear cut when you're trying to allocate them into a category of expenses.

One common behavioral pattern people face is impulse spending. They see something they like on the shelf, and involuntary action makes them reach out for it - without even taking a look at the price tag.

Yet there are ways to curb impulse spending:

🏛 The Time Out Rule - When you see something you want to purchase, take a breath and wait for a certain period of time before you proceed with the purchase. In fact, the longer you wait, the better. If you still feel strongly about it by the end of the time-out period, you may consider doing so - but only after making sure you have the funds or budget to do so!

🏛 The Spending Pattern - You may realize you tend to splurge when you're at the mall or when you're shopping online. Stop yourself from zeroing in on the mall when you feel upset or when you get your paycheck. Change your spending pattern: Go to the park for a short hike or meet a friend for a swim. If you're notorious for spending excessively when shopping online, set a block on your web browsers, or set a up a reward-based system to reward yourself for keeping your impulses in check!

🏛 The Never-Ending Sales - Just as you should be aware of your spending pattern, you should be aware of your impulses where sales are concerned. Don't be fooled by sales. Those with huge markdowns can make it very tempting to put it on the cart. But before you convince yourself of the savings you'll make from the purchase, stop and ask yourself: Do you REALLY need it?

The Vision Board - Refer to your Vision Board from "The Richest Man In Babylon" and keep in mind your end-goals or dreams. Keep in mind how your impulse spending will affect your goals!

THE THIRD CURE

MAKE THY GOLD MULTIPLY.

"Behold thy lean purse is fattening. Thou hast disciplined thyself to leave therein one-tenth of all thou earneth. Thou hast controlled thy expenditures to protect thy growing treasure. Next, we will consider means to put thy treasure to labor and to increase. Gold in a purse is gratifying to own and satisfieth a miserly soul but earns nothing. The gold we may retain from our earnings is but the start.

The earnings it will make shall build our fortunes." So spoke Arkad upon the third day to his class.

"How therefore may we put our gold to work? My first investment was unfortunate, for I lost all. Its tale I will relate later. My first profitable investment was a loan I made to a man named Aggar, a shield maker. Once each year did he buy large shipments of bronze brought from across the sea to use in his trade. Lacking sufficient capital to pay the merchants, he would borrow from those who had extra coins. He was an honorable man. His borrowing he would repay, together with a liberal rental, as he sold his shields.

"Each time I loaned to him I loaned back also the rental he had paid to me. Therefore not only did my capital increase, but its earnings likewise increased. Most gratifying was it to have these sums return to my purse.

"I tell you, my students, a man's wealth is not in the coins he carries in his purse; it is the income he buildeth, the golden stream that continually floweth into his purse and keepeth it always bulging.

That is what every man desireth. That is what thou, each one of thee desireth; an income that continueth to come whether thou work or travel.

"Great income I have acquired. So great that I am called a very rich man. My loans to Aggar were my first training in profitable investment. Gaining wisdom from this experience, I extended my loans and investments as my capital increased. From a few sources at first, from many sources later, flowed into my purse a golden stream of wealth available for such wise uses as I should decide.

"Behold, from my humble earnings I had begotten a hoard of golden slaves, each laboring and earning more gold. As they labored for me, so their children also labored and their children's children until great was the income from their combined efforts.

"Gold increaseth rapidly when making reasonable earnings as thou wilt see from the following:

A farmer, when his first son was born, took ten pieces of silver to a money lender and asked him to keep it on rental for his son until he became twenty years of age. This the money lender did, and agreed the rental should be one-fourth of its value each four years. The farmer asked, because this sum he had set aside as belonging to his son, that the rental be add to the principal.

"When the boy had reached the age of twenty years, the farmer again went to the money lender to inquire about the silver. The money lender explained that because this sum had been increased by compound interest, the original ten pieces of silver had now grown to thirty and one-half pieces.

"The farmer was well pleased and because the son did not need the coins, he left them with the money lender.

When the son became fifty years of age, the father meantime having passed to the other world, the money lender paid the son in settlement one hundred and sixty-seven pieces of silver.

"Thus in fifty years had the investment multiplied itself at rental almost seventeen times.

"This, then, is the third cure for a lean purse: to put each coin to laboring that it may reproduce its kind even as the flocks of the field and help bring to thee income, a stream of wealth that shall flow constantly into thy purse."

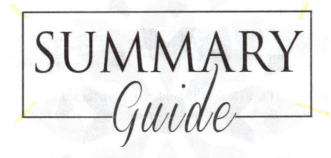

On the third day, Arkad's lesson was to put into use the growing treasure which was accumulated from the first 2 Cures.

He related his first profitable experience of making a loan. Aggar was a shield maker, and he often need to borrow large sums of money to pay the sea-faring merchants for the equally large shipments of bronze. By loaning the money to Aggar, who would repay him back once he made and sold the bronze shields, Arkad essentially made good on his investment.

He related another example to the chosen hundred:

A farmer, at the birth of his first born, deposited 10 pieces of silver with a money lender. The latter offered an interest term of 1/4 a silver's value every 4 years. The farmer agreed, stating that the interest would be added on to the principal amount, and only redeemable when his son turned 20 years of age.

When 20 years passed, the farmer approached the moneylender and was pleased to learn that the original principal sum had grown to 30 and a half pieces of silver!

Yet, the farmer continued leaving it with the moneylender since his son did not need the money. Eventually, when the son reached 50 years of age, and the farmer already passed on, the former received a total of 167 pieces of silver from the moneylender.

LEARNING/LESSON

For Arkad's third Cure (Make thy gold multiply), the underlying principle is making loans. For his part, he loaned money directly to Aggar for his business.

At the same time, it also happened in his anecdote to the chosen hundred. Although the farmer passed the silver to the moneylender, he was in effect also a moneylender. The moneylender usually liaised with businesses in short of money so therefore the farmer was essentially investing in businesses.

Of course, we're not telling you here to be a moneylender. Today, the bank has taken over the role of a (legitimate) moneylender. Generally though, the interest rates for deposits in the bank would hardly make significant returns.

In modern financial terms, loans are known as a form of debt instrument.

Besides loans, debt instruments include bonds (corporate, municipal, treasury), certificates, leases, mortgages, notes or any other agreements between a lender and a borrower.

You may have heard of Kickstarter. Essentially, it is a global crowdfunding platform based here in the States.

Everyone is able to back listed projects, and are offered tangible rewards based on the amount they pledge, which is also technically a form of loan, or investment. However, in this case, the rewards are mostly tangible rewards towards specific items, and are not towards securing a passive income.

For the purpose of this book, let's talk about proper investing, specifically, in a small business.
Here, a small business refers to a company which is founded from scratch. For a small business, there are basically 2 ways of investment - equity and debt.

🏛 **Equity Investment** - An equity investment generally refers to the purchase of a ownership stake in the company. This investment is usually provided in the form of cash, in exchange for the company's profits, and losses, in a proportional manner. With this investment, the company can use it for expansion, debt reduction, hire new staff, etc.

🏛 **Debt Investment** A debt investment refers to the loan to the company in exchange of for the promise of interest income, together with the eventual repayment of the principal amount. In the event that the company goes bust, the debt has priority over the equity investors.

On the whole, debt investments are seen to be a lower-risk investment. However, they run against a particular risk - inflation.

Often, many debt-based investments offer a rate of return which is lower than the rate of inflation. Therefore, the longer you hold on to them, the lower the value of your investment sum.

The exercise for this chapter is for you to:

🏛 **Step 1**: Look up the companies that you're interested in and looking at their overall performance over the years.

🏛 **Step 2**: Discuss with a qualified broker or dealer and make an informed decision.

THE FOURTH CURE

GUARD THY TREASURES FROM LOSS.

"Misfortune loves a shining mark. Gold in a man's purse must be guarded with firmness, else it be lost. Thus it is wise that we must first secure small amounts and learn to protect them before the Gods entrust us with larger." So spoke Arkad upon the fourth day to his class.

"Every owner of gold is tempted by opportunities whereby it would seem that he could make large sums by its investment in most plausible projects. Often friends and relatives are eagerly entering such investment and urge him to follow.

"The first sound principle of investment is security for thy principal. Is it wise to be intrigued by larger earnings when thy principal may be lost? I say not. The penalty of risk is probable loss. Study carefully, before parting with thy treasure, each assurance that it may be safely reclaimed. Be not misled by thine own romantic desires to make wealth rapidly.

"Before thou loan it to any man assure thyself of his ability to repay and his reputation for doing so, that thou mayest not unwittingly be making him a present of thy hard-earned treasure.

"Before thou entrust it as an investment in any field acquaint thyself with the dangers which may beset it.

"My own first investment was a tragedy to me at the time. The guarded savings of a year I did entrust to a brick maker, named Azmur, who was traveling over the far seas and in Tyre agreed to buy for me the rare jewels of the Phoenicians. These we would sell upon his return and divide the profits.

77

The Phoenicians were scoundrels and sold him bits of glass. My treasure was lost. Today, my training would show to me at once the folly of entrusting a brick maker to buy jewels.

"Therefore, do I advise thee from the wisdom of my experiences: be not too confident of thine own wisdom in entrusting thy treasures to the possible pitfalls of investments. Better by far to consult the wisdom of those experienced in handling money for profit. Such advice is freely given for the asking and may readily possess a value equal in gold to the sum thou considerest investing. In truth, such is its actual value if it save thee from loss.

"This, then, is the fourth cure for a lean purse, and of great importance if it prevent thy purse from being emptied once it has become well filled."

"Guard thy treasure from loss by investing only where thy principal is safe, where it may be reclaimed if desirable, and where thou will not fail to collect a fair rental. Consult with wise men. Secure the advice of those experienced in the profitable handling of gold. Let their wisdom protect thy treasure from unsafe investments."

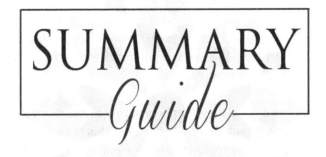
SUMMARY Guide

On the fourth day, Arkad's spoke about misfortune.

His reasoning was that people who have gold with them would be tempted to do many things with it, including investment. However, plenty of risk made it entirely possible for the whole fortune to be lost.

He related his experience of investing his savings with Azmur a brick maker who sought to buy rare jewels. At that point he should be concerned. A brick maker who was well versed in buying jewels?

But Arkad trusted him, and as expected his fortune was lost, because Azmur was sold worthless glass and he was unable to discern the trickery until too late.

LEARNING/LESSON

What is the learning lesson?

Simple - Do not be taken in by rosy-sounding deals. If it sounds too good to be true, it probably is.

For some people, they prefer to rely on themselves and they take it upon themselves to learn about the industries they were interested n investing.

For some people, they prefer to cut the hassle to the minimum and instead to rely on others. There is no right or wrong to this, only your preference. If you prefer to seek the advice of professionals, do make sure that they are experienced enough.

However, for some people, they simply turn to the ones nearest to them - their friends, family members or the partner. This is one of the biggest mistakes because these people are usually not experts at all! (Unless they are indeed trained professionals in the respective industry).

Here's a cautionary tale courtesy of Baltimore Colts quarterback Johnny Unitas (May 7, 1933 - September 11, 2002).

Johnny Unitas had a successful career from the 1950s to the 1970s. He was the NFL's MVP for 1959, 1964 and 1967. In addition, he held the record for the most consecutive games with a touchdown pass for a whooping 52 years, before New Orleans Saints quarterback Drew Brees broke it in 2012.

After his career, Johnny Unitas invested his money in many ventures, such as an air freight company, bowling alleys, real estate, restaurants, and the like.

But because his forte was in football, all his ventures went down the drain, and he even had to file for bankruptcy in 1991. So, as you can see, no one is immune to misfortune, or bad decision.

To guard against loss, you need to make critical and sound decisions, and here are the steps to that:

> 🏛 **The Situational Analysis** - Say for example you're in a situation where you need to make an investment to grow your wealth. Therefore you need to have all the necessary data before you to make an informed decision.

At the same time, realize that your decision may have an impact on people around you, maybe your loved one or the business partner etc, so consider such consequences before you pull the trigger on any decision.

🏛 **The Benefit/Cost Analysis** - What are the potential benefits? What are the expected costs (besides the investment sum)? What if the benefits fall below of expectation? What if the expected costs exceed expectation?

🏛 **The Reward/Risk Ratio** - What is the risk factor? Is it stacked against you or are the odds in your favor?

🏛 **The Assessment** - Based on your values and beliefs, make an assessment on the analysis. Importantly your values and beliefs should not be compromised in any way. What you need to do is to stand firmly behind your assessment.

🏛 **The Decision** - The final step of your analysis. This is where you must be willing to take the step forward and take action. Investment decisions can often be time-sensitive, so if you wait too long to seize it, it may no longer be viable. So even if you don't have a complete set of data to work with, you must make a decision - to make a decision!

BONUS: The Back Up Plan - Plan B.

Do you have one when you realize you made a wrong decision? Is there anything you can fall back on? Is anything else implicated in a supposed failure? Therefore it is important that there is a contingency plan.

THE FIFTH CURE

MAKE OF THY DWELLING A PROFITABLE INVESTMENT.

"If a man setteth aside nine parts of his earnings upon which to live and enjoy life, and if any part of this nine parts he can turn into a profitable investment without detriment to his wellbeing, then so much faster will his treasures grow." So spake Arkad to his class at their fifth lesson.

"All too many of our men of Babylon do raise their families in unseemly quarters. They do pay to exacting landlords liberal rentals for rooms where their wives have not a spot to raise the blooms that gladden a woman's heart and their children have no place to play their games except in the unclean alleys.

"No man's family can fully enjoy life unless they do have a plot of ground wherein children can play in the clean earth and where the wife may raise not only blossoms but good rich herbs to feed her family.

"To a man's heart it brings gladness to eat the figs from his own trees and the grapes of his own vines. To own his own domicile and to have it a place he is proud to care for, putteth confidence in his heart and greater effort behind all his endeavors. Therefore, do I recommend that every man own the roof that sheltereth him and his.

"Nor is it beyond the ability of any well intentioned man to own his home.

Hath not our great king so widely extended the walls of Babylon that within them much land is now 48unused and may be purchased at sums most reasonable?

"Also I say to you, my students, that the money lenders gladly consider the desires of men who seek homes and land for their families. Readily may thou borrow to pay the brick maker and the builder for such commendable purposes, if thou can show a reasonable portion of the necessary sum which thou thyself hath provided for the purpose.

"Then when the house be built, thou canst pay the money lender with the same regularity as thou didst pay the landlord. Because each payment will
reduce thy indebtedness to the money lender, a few years will satisfy his loan.

"Then will thy heart be glad because thou wilt own in thy own right a valuable property and thy only cost will be the king's taxes.

"Also wilt thy good wife go more often to the river to wash thy robes, that each time returning she may bring a goatskin of water to pour upon the growing things.

"Thus come many blessings to the man who owneth his own house. And greatly will it reduce his cost of living, making available more of his earnings for pleasures and the gratification of his desires. This, then, is the fifth cure for a lean purse: Own thy own home"

SUMMARY
Guide

On the fifth day, Arkad's spoke about dwelling.

According to his observation, the people of Babylon were living in "unseemly quarters". Because it was all rental, families were unable to live in complete ease. Therefore he recommended to the chosen hundred that they own their place. This was possible because the land was available for a reasonable price. At the same time, the moneylenders were also willing to loan them the money, at a reasonable interest rate, to pay the brick makers.

Eventually, after the repayment, they would fully owned their houses and there would be no need to pay to the landlord anymore.

LEARNING / LESSON

What is the learning lesson here?

Generally, when you rent a place, you continuously make payments to stay there.

When you purchase a home, you may also need to make payments to the moneylender whom you loaned the money to make the purchase.

However once you cleared the payments, the house belongs to you, and you don't have to pay for it anymore (except for the recurring miscellaneous fees or others). Once cleared, a bigger portion of your earnings is now available for other uses.

Here are some considerations for renting or owning:

Consideration For Renting	Consideration For Owning
No funds for a down payment	Intend to live there for a few years
Income may not be stable	Have a stable income
Housing need may change accordingly	Housing need is stable
Possible change in career, requiring a move in a few years	No change in career
No intention to improve the appearance or structure of the house	Intention to improve the appearance or structure of the house
No intention to handle any general maintenance of the house	Intention to benefit from the income tax benefits of the house ownership

In the time of Arkad, owning a home was a more straightforward process.

In today's climate, things are more different and varied. There are definitely exceptions where it may be better to rent. However for the purpose of The Richest Man In Babylon, I would like for you to own your place!

Here are the basics that you need to know:

🏛 **The Down Payment** - This amount is usually paid in cash, and it constitutes about 3.5 to 20% of the sale price of the house.

🏛 **The Rest Of The Payment** - This amount is usually settled by a loan from a bank known as the mortgage. This means you need to repay it to the bank, inclusive of the interest. It requires usually about 15 to 30 years for full repayment.

🏛 **The Monthly Payment** - Usually hovers around 0.75 to 1.15% of the purchase price. (Taking the example of $205,200 from the NAR report, 1.15% is calculated to be $2,359.80). This is just an initial amount, and does not take into account the closing costs and miscellaneous costs.

According to a report Metro Home Prices Maintain Steady Growth In First Quarter Of 2015, by the National Association of Realtors (NAR), home prices in metro areas during the first quarter of 2015 have increased due to strong demand (despite lagging inventory levels).

"The national median existing single-family home price in the first quarter was $205,200, up 7.4 percent from the first quarter of 2014 ($191,100)."

Assuming you made an approximate gauge and you are sure you can afford to own a place, here are the action steps:

🏛 **Step 1**: Get a copy of your credit report and clean up your credit to the best of your abilities.

🏛 **Step 2**: Approach a bank officer to fill out an application for a pre-qual letter. (There may be an application fee).

🏛 **Step 3**: Approach a real estate agent to recommend the houses available according to your budget etc.

🏛 **Step 4**: Obtain a Disclosure from the seller of the house that you decide on. This Disclosure will present the existing problems of the house, as required by law.

🏛 **Step 5**: Make an offer. (You may consult your agent etc).

🏛 **Step 6**: Sign a contract when a seller agrees to your price. This agreement will basically cement both parties' obligation to sell or buy.

🏛 **Step 7**: Engage a professional inspection of the house. This will uncover any additional problems with the house, that you may then re-negotiate with the seller to lower the price.

🏛 **Step 8**: The bank will arrange for an appraisal/inspection of the house to ascertain that you're paying for what it is worth.

🏛 **Step 9**: Approach an insurance officer to clarify the insurance amount. Obtain comparisons if possible.

🏛 **Step 10**: Once the contract is signed, the company handling the closing will finalize the paperwork.

And before long, you'll get your own place!

THE SIXTH CURE

INSURE A FUTURE INCOME.

"The life of every man proceedeth from his childhood to his old age. This is the path of life and no man may deviate from it unless the Gods call him prematurely to the world beyond. Therefore do I say that it behooves a man to make preparation for a suitable income in the days to come, when he is no longer young, and to make preparations for his family should he be no longer with them to comfort and support them. This lesson shall instruct thee in providing a full purse when time has made thee less able to learn." So Arkad addressed his class upon the sixth day.

"The man who, because of his understanding of the laws of wealth, acquireth a growing surplus, should give thought to those future days. He should plan certain investments or provision that may endure safely for many years, yet will be available when the time arrives which he has so wisely anticipated.

"There are diverse ways by which a man may provide with safety for his future. He may provide a hiding place and there bury a secret treasure. Yet, no matter with what skill it be hidden, it may nevertheless become the loot of thieves. For this reason I recommend not this plan.

"A man may buy houses or lands for this purpose. If wisely chosen as to their usefulness and value in the future, they are permanent in their value and their earnings or their sale will provide well for his purpose.

"A man may loan a small sum to the money lender and increase it at regular periods. The rental which the money lender adds to this will largely add to its increase.

I do know a sandal maker, named Ansan, who explained to me not long ago that each week for eight years he had deposited with his money lender two pieces of silver. The money lender had but recently given him an accounting over which he greatly rejoiced. The total of his small deposits with their rental at the customary rate of one-fourth their value for each four years, had now become a thousand and forty pieces of silver.

"I did gladly encourage him further by demonstrating to him with my knowledge of the numbers that in twelve years more, if he would keep his regular deposits of but two pieces of silver each week, the money lender would then owe him four thousand pieces of silver, a worthy competence for the rest of his life.

"Surely, when such a small payment made with regularity doth produce such profitable results, no man can afford not to insure a treasure for his old age and the protection of his family, no matter how prosperous his business and his investments may be.

"I would that I might say more about this. In my mind rests a belief that some day wise-thinking men will devise a plan to insure against death whereby many men pay in but a trifling sum regularly, the aggregate making a handsome sum for the family of each member who passeth to the beyond. This do I see as something desirable and which I could highly recommend.

But today it is not possible because it must reach beyond the life of any man or any partnership to operate. It must be as stable as the King's throne.

Some day do I feel that such a plan shall come to pass and be a great blessing to many men, because even the first small payment will make available a snug fortune for the family of a member should he pass on.

"But because we live in our own day and not in the days which are to come, must we take advantage of those means and ways of accomplishing our purposes.

Therefore do I recommend to all men, that they, by wise and well thought out methods, do provide against a lean purse in their mature years. For a lean purse to a man no longer able to earn or to a family without its head is a sore tragedy.

"This, then, is the sixth cure for a lean purse. Provide in advance for the needs of thy growing age and the protection of thy family."

SUMMARY
Guide

On the sixth day, Arkad addressed the issue of mortality. With the usual aging of a man, he may not be able to work any longer. Therefore he ought to consider his own future so that he may be still accessible to wealth when he can no longer work. At the same time, a man also should anticipate the family's financial needs when he has passed on.

He related a few ways to insure a future income. First, a man may buy houses or lands and wisely make use of them. Secondly, a man may loan a sum of money to the moneylender and reap from it. In fact Arkad essentially predicted the concept of life insurance because he came up with the idea that the best situation of an insured future is such that there will be a regular payment to the family even when the head of the family passed on.

LEARNING/LESSON

Essentially, many strategies can ensure a future income.

From the Learning Lessons so far, we've actually covered a few of them, such as investment plans, savings plans etc, that in some way will provide a future income.

Although we have 2 scenarios here (retirement and death), we basically need the same thing - a source of income to cover the life of the person (retirement) or that of the family (death of breadwinner).

A well-known example comes from Whitney Houston (Aug 9, 1963 - February 11, 2012).

Since she burst into the R&B scene in 1983, she had amassed a multimillion-dollar fortune. However by Jan 2012, it was reported that her fortune was gone.

It was also reported that Whitney Houston was reduced to asking friends for money, for instance, Clive Davis in February, prior to her death. Her home was near to being repossessed and she was in financial ruin.

Yet she managed to leave behind a $20 million legacy for her daughter Bobbi Kristina, although the fate of the inheritance is now in doubt due to an incident that left the latter unresponsive in hospital (at the time of this writing).

Generally speaking, for insurance policies, you would have to list down the beneficiaries in order to eliminate any contentious issues.

Writing a will is actually very useful, although most people seem resistant toward it, and tend to shy away from what they perceive to be a taboo topic. But it is something that is very relevant in today's climate, as it safeguards your family or loved one's future.

Here in the States, the actual procedure may differ from state to state.

Here are basic steps to creating a will:

🏛 **Choose An Executor** - The executor will settle the estate after the death of the individual. This includes taking inventory of assets and property, distributing it, paying taxes or debts owed by the deceased etc. The executor should be over the age of 18, not previously convicted of a felony charge and of sound mind. It may be the family accountant, a lawyer, a spouse or even a friend.

🏛 **Choose Beneficiary** - The beneficiary will inherit whatever is listed in the will. Secondary or contingent beneficiary nomination may be necessary.

 You may access this link to find out more:
http://www.usa.gov/topics/money/personal-finance/wills.shtml

THE SEVENTH CURE

INCREASE THY ABILITY TO EARN

"This day do I speak to thee, my students, of one of the most vital remedies for a lean purse.

Yet, I will talk not of gold but of yourselves, of the men beneath the robes of many colors who do sit before me. I will talk to you of those things within the minds and lives of men which do work for or against their success." So did Arkad address his class upon the seventh day.

"Not long ago came to me a young man seeking to borrow. When I questioned him the cause of his necessity, he complained that his earnings were insufficient to pay his expenses. Thereupon I explained to him, this being the case, he was a poor customer for the money lender, as he possessed no surplus earning capacity to repay the loan.

"What you need, young man,' I told him, 'is to earn more coins. What dost thou to increase thy capacity to earn?'

"All that I can do' he replied. 'Six times within two moons have I approached my master to request my pay be increased, but without success. No man can go oftener than that."

"We may smile at his simplicity, yet he did possess one of the vital requirements to increase his earnings. Within him was a strong desire to earn more, a proper and commendable desire.

"Preceding accomplishment must be desire. Thy desires must be strong and definite. General desires are but weak longings. For a man to wish to be rich is of little purpose.

For a man to desire five pieces of gold is a tangible desire which he can press to fulfillment. After he has backed his desire for five pieces of gold with strength of purpose to secure it, next he can find similar ways to obtain ten pieces and then twenty pieces and later a thousand pieces and, behold, he has become wealthy. In learning to secure his one definite small desire, he hath trained himself to secure a larger one. This is the process by which wealth is accumulated: first in small sums, then in larger ones as a man learns and becomes more capable.

"Desires must be simple and definite. They defeat their own purpose should they be too many, too confusing, or beyond a man's training to accomplish."

As a man perfecteth himself in his calling even so doth his ability to earn increase. In those days when I was a humble scribe carving upon the clay for a few coppers each day, I observed that other workers did more than I and were paid more. Therefore, did I determine that I would be exceeded by none. Nor did it take long for me to discover the reason for their greater success.

More interest in my work, more concentration upon my task, more persistence in my effort, and, behold, few men could carve more tablets in a day than I. With reasonable promptness my increased skill was rewarded, nor was it necessary for me to go six times to my master to request recognition.

"The more of wisdom we know, the more we may earn. That man who seeks to learn more of his craft shall be richly rewarded. If he is an artisan, he may seek to learn the methods and the tools of those most skillful in the same line.

If he laboreth at the law or at healing, he may consult and exchange knowledge with others of his calling. If he be a merchant, he may continually seek better goods that can be purchased at lower prices.

"Always do the affairs of man change and improve because keen-minded men seek greater skill that they may better serve those upon whose patronage they depend. Therefore, I urge all men to be in the front rank of progress and not to stand still, lest they be left behind.

"Many things come to make a man's life rich with gainful experiences. Such things as the following, a man must do if he respect himself:

"He must pay his debts with all the promptness within his power, not purchasing that for which he is unable to pay.

"He must take care of his family that they may think and speak well of him. "He must make a will of record that, in case the Gods call him, proper and honorable division of his property be accomplished.

"He must have compassion upon those who are injured and smitten by misfortune and aid them within reasonable limits. He must do deeds of thoughtfulness to those dear to him.

"Thus the seventh and last remedy for a lean purse is to cultivate thy own powers, to study and become wiser, to become more skillful, to so act as to
respect thyself. Thereby shalt thou acquire confidence in thy self to achieve thy carefully considered desires.

"These then are the seven cures for a lean purse, which, out of the experience of a long and successful life, I do urge for all men who desire wealth. "There is more gold in Babylon, my students, than thou dreamest of. There is abundance for all.

"Go thou forth and practice these truths that thou mayest prosper and grow wealthy, as is thy right.

"Go thou forth and teach these truths that every honorable subject of his majesty may also share liberally in the ample wealth of our beloved city."

SUMMARY Guide

On the seventh day, Arkad's class to the chosen hundred came full circle. After talking about gold and investment and other related aspects, he now returned to the person himself.

Arkad related a story where a young man came to borrow money from him. The latter revealed that his expenses exceeded his earnings, and that he even spoke to his master but to no avail. To Arkad, he earnestly spoke of his desire to learn.

And the lesson came from that - the desire to learn.

To Arkad, the desire to learn and improve and be more skillful acts as a way to manifest success beyond the usual aspects.

With that, Arkad called forth the chosen hundred to practice the Cures and to spread it so that every man of Babylon can achieve success like he did.

LEARNING/LESSON

What is the learning lesson here? It is expertly explained here:

"The more of wisdom we know, the more we may earn. That man who seeks to learn more of his craft shall be richly rewarded. If he is an artisan, he may seek to learn the methods and the tools of those most skillful in the same line.

If he laboreth at the law or at healing, he may consult and exchange knowledge with others of his calling. If he be a merchant, he may continually seek better goods that can be purchased at lower prices."

In today's world, if you are able to enhance your knowledge through constant learning, you will have an edge over others, which will obviously give you more of a head start in manifesting wealth and success.

To be an effective learner, check out the following tips to enhance your learning ability!

- 🏛 **Memory Enhancement** - When you study something, focus on it. By clearly focusing, the information will be transferred from the short-term memory to the long-term storage bank. Avoid distractions like the TV, music etc.

- 🏛 **Multiple Way Learning** - Learn in multiple ways because it can further consolidate the learning in your mind. For instance, use your 5 senses to enhance the process; draw out a mind map on a piece of paper, or watch instructional videos.

- 🏛 **Teach Another** - The best way to know if you've learned anything, correctly, is to teach someone else.

When you first learned the knowledge, you essentially assimilated it in your own terms and understood it through your own unique thought processes. Through that refined understanding, you now pass on your knowledge to another.

- 🏛 **Gain Practical Experience** - In learning new things, the knowledge must also be applied in real life. Only then can the learning be reinforced and improved.

BONUS TIP - Keep On Learning.

Don't think that once you start working, you no longer have the need to learn. Whether you are still in school, or you're out in the working world, never stop learning. It is the best way to keep your brain active and create new neural networks that help expand your mind.

By keeping the brain active, it ensures a healthier mind and life. At the same time, you value-add your skills as you learn, and this essentially you get to earn more!

IMPORTANT!

Don't forget to download your special gift for these Seven Cures called **"Affirmations for Affluence"** at:

www.RichestManDecoded.com/bonus

MEET THE GODDESS OF GOOD LUCK.

IF a man Be LUCKY, THeRe IS no FoReTeLLING THe POSSIBLe eXTeNT OF HIS GOOD FORTUNe. PITCH HIM INTO THe euPHRaTes anD LIKe aS NOT He WILL SWIM OUT WITH a PeaRL In HIS HanD.

—Babylonian Proverb

The desire to be lucky is universal. It was just as strong in the breasts of men four thousand years ago in ancient Babylon as it is in the hearts of men today. We all hope to be favored by the whimsical Goddess of Good Luck.

Is there some way we can meet her and attract, not only her favorable attention, but her generous favors? Is there a way to attract good luck? That is just what the men of ancient Babylon wished to know. It is exactly what they decided to find out. They were shrewd men and keen thinkers. That explains why their city became the richest and most powerful city of their time.

In that distant past, they had no schools or colleges. Nevertheless they had a center of learning and a very practical one it was. Among the towered buildings in Babylon was one that ranked in importance with the Palace of the King, the Hanging Gardens and the temples of the Gods.

You will find scant mention of it in the history books, more likely no mention at all, yet it exerted a powerful influence upon the thought of that time.

This building was the Temple of Learning where the wisdom of the past was expounded by voluntary teachers and where subjects of popular interest were discussed in open forums.

Within its walls all men met as equals. The humblest of slaves could dispute with impunity the opinions of a prince of the royal house.

Among the many who frequented the Temple of Learning, was a wise rich man named Arkad, called the richest man in Babylon. He had his own special hall where almost any evening a large group of men, some old, some very young, but mostly middle-aged, gathered to discuss and argue interesting subjects. Suppose we listen in to see whether they knew how to attract good luck.

The sun had just set like a great red ball of fire shining through the haze of desert dust when Arkad strolled to his accustomed platform. Already full four score men were awaiting his arrival, reclining on their small rugs spread upon the floor. More were still arriving.

"What shall we discuss this night?" Arkad inquired.

After a brief hesitation, a tall cloth weaver addressed him, arising as was the custom. "I have a subject I would like to hear discussed yet hesitate to offer lest it seem ridiculous to you, Arkad, and my good friends here."

Upon being urged to offer it, both by Arkad and by calls from the others, he continued: "This day I have been lucky, for I have found a purse in which there are pieces of gold. To continue to be lucky is my great desire. Feeling that all men share with me this desire, I do suggest we debate how to attract good luck that we may discover ways it can be enticed to one."

"A most interesting subject has been offered, Arkad commented, "one most worthy of our discussion.

To some men, good luck bespeaks but a chance happening that, like an accident, may befall one without purpose or reason. Others do believe that the instigator of all good fortune is our most bounteous goddess, Ashtar, ever anxious to reward with generous gifts those who please her. Speak up, my friends, what say you, shall we seek to find if there be means by which good luck may be enticed to visit each and all of us?"

"Yea! Yea! And much of it!" responded the growing group of eager listeners.

Thereupon Arkad continued, "To start our discussion, let us first hear from those among us who have enjoyed experiences similar to that of the cloth weaver in finding or receiving, without effort upon their part, valuable treasures or jewels."

There was a pause in which all looked about expecting someone to reply but no one did.

"What, no one?" Arkad said, "then rare indeed must be this kind of good luck. Who now will offer a suggestion as to where we shall continue our search?" That I will do," spoke a well-robed young man, arising. "When a man speaketh of luck is it not natural that his thoughts turn to the gaining tables? Is it not there we find many men courting the favour of the goddess in hope she will bless them with rich winnings?"

As he resumed his seat a voice called, "Do not stop! Continue thy story! Tell us, didst thou find favor with the goddess at the gaming tables? Did she turn the cubes with red side up so thou filled thy purse at the dealer's expense or did she permit the blue sides to come up so the dealer raked in thy hard-earned pieces of silver?"

The young man joined the good-natured laughter, then replied, "I am not averse to admitting she seemed not to know I was even there. But how about the rest of you?

Have you found her waiting about such places to roll the cubes, in your favor? We are eager to hear as well as to learn."

"A wise start," broke in Arkad. "We meet here to consider all sides of each question. To ignore the gaming table would be to overlook an instinct common to most men, the love of taking a chance with a small amount of silver in the hope of winning much gold."

"That doth remind me of the races but yesterday," called out another listener. "If the goddess frequents the gaming tables, certainly she dost not overlook the races where the gilded chariots and the foaming horses offer far more excitement. Tell us honestly, Arkad, didst she whisper to you to place your bet upon those grey horses from Nineveh yesterday? I was standing just behind thee and could scarce believe my ears when I heard thee place thy bet upon the greys. Thou knowest as well as any of us that no team in all Assyria can beat our beloved bays in a fair race.

"Didst the goddess whisper in thy ear to bet upon the greys because at the last turn the inside black would stumble and so interfere with our bays that the greys would win the race and score an unearned victory?"

Arkad smiled indulgently at the banter. "What reason have we to feel the good goddess would take that much interest in any man's bet upon a horse race? To me she is a goddess of love and dignity whose pleasure it is to aid those who are in need and to reward those who are deserving. I look to find her, not at the gaming tables or the races where men lose more gold than they win but in other places where the doings of men are more worthwhile and more worthy of reward.

"In tilling the soil, in honest trading, in all of man's occupations, there is opportunity to make a profit upon his efforts and his transactions.

Perhaps not all the time will he be rewarded because sometimes his judgment may be faulty and other times the winds and the weather may defeat his efforts. Yet, if he persists, he may usually expect to realize his profit. This is so because the chances of profit are always in his favor.

"But, when a man playeth the games, the situation is reversed for the chances of profit are always against him and always in favor of the game keeper. The game is so arranged that it will always favor the keeper. It is his business at which he plans to make a liberal profit for himself from the coins bet by the players. Few players realize how certain are the game keeper's profits and how uncertain are their own chances to win.

"For example, let us consider wagers placed upon the cube. Each time it is cast we bet which side will be uppermost. If it be the red side the game master pays to us four times our bet. But if any other of the five sides come uppermost, we lose our bet.

Thus the figures show that for each cast we have five chances to lose, but because the red pays four for one, we have four chances to win. In a night's play the game master can expect to keep for his profit one-fifth of all the coins wagered. Can a man expect to win more than occasionally against odds so arranged that he should lose one-fifth of all his bets?"

"Yet some men do win large sums at times," volunteered one of the listeners.

"Quite so, they do," Arkad continued. "Realizing this, the question comes to me whether money secured in such ways brings permanent value to those who are thus lucky. Among my acquaintances are many of the successful men of Babylon, yet among them I am unable to name a single one who started his success from such a source.

"You who are gathered here tonight know many more of our substantial citizens. To me it would be of much interest to learn how many of our successful citizens can credit the gaming tables with their start to success. Suppose each of you tell of those you know. What say you?"

103

After a prolonged silence, a wag ventured, 'Wouldst thy inquiry include the game keepers?" "If you think of no one else," Arkad responded.

"If not one of you can think of anyone else, then how about yourselves? Are there any consistent winners with us who hesitate to advise such a source for their incomes?"

His challenge was answered by a series of groans from the rear taken up and spread amid much laughter.

"It would seem we are not seeking good luck in such places as the goddess frequents," he continued. "Therefore let us explore other fields. We have not found it in picking up lost wallets.

Neither have we found it haunting the gaming tables. As to the races, I must confess to have lost far more coins there than I have ever won.

"Now, suppose we consider our trades and businesses. Is it not natural if we conclude a profitable transaction to consider it not good luck but a just reward for our efforts? I am inclined to think we may be overlooking the gifts of the goddess. Perhaps she really does assist us when we do not appreciate her generosity. Who can suggest further discussion?"

Thereupon an elderly merchant arose, smoothing his genteel white robe. "With thy permission, most honorable Arkad and my friends, I offer a suggestion. If, as you have said, we take credit to our own industry and ability for our business success, why not consider the successes we almost enjoyed but which escaped us, happenings which would have been most profitable.

They would have been rare examples of good luck if they had actually happened. Because they were not brought to fulfillment we cannot consider them as our just rewards. Surely many men here have such experiences to relate."

"Here is a wise approach," Arkad approved. "Who among you have had good luck within your grasp only to see it escape?"

Many hands were raised, among them that of the merchant. Arkad motioned to him to speak.

"As you suggested this approach, we should like to hear first from you."

"I will gladly relate a tale," he resumed, "that doth illustrate how closely unto a man good luck may approach and how blindly he may permit it to escape, much to his loss and later regret.

"Many years ago, when I was a young man, just married and well-started to earning, my father did come one day and urge most strongly that I enter in an investment. The son of one of his good friends had taken notice of a barren tract of land not far beyond the outer walls of our city. It lay high above the canal where no water could reach it.

"The son of my father's friend devised a plan to purchase this land, build three large water wheels that could be operated by oxen and thereby raise the life-giving waters to the fertile soil. This accomplished, he planned to divide into small tracts and sell to the residents of the city for herb patches.

"The son of my father's friend did not possess sufficient gold to complete such an undertaking. Like myself, he was a young man earning a fair sum. His father, like mine, was a man of large family and small means. He, therefore, decided to interest a group of men to enter the enterprise with him.

The group was to comprise twelve, each of whom must be a money earner and agree to pay one-tenth of his earnings into the enterprise until the land was made ready for sale. All would then share justly in the profits in proportion to their investment."

'Thou, my son,' bespoke my father unto me, 'art now in thy young manhood. It is my deep desire that thou begin the building of a valuable estate for myself that thou mayest become respected among men. I desire to see thou profit from a knowledge of the thoughtless mistakes of thy father."

This do I most ardently desire, my father,' I replied.

"Then, this do I advise. Do what I should have done at thy age. From thy earnings keep out one-tenth to put into favorable investments. With this one-tenth of thy earnings and what it will also earn, thou canst, before thou art my age, accumulate for thyself a valuable estate.

"Thy words are words of wisdom, my father. Greatly do I desire riches. Yet there are many uses to which my earnings are called. Therefore, do I hesitate to do as thou dost advise. I am young.

There is plenty of time.'

"So I thought at thy age, yet behold, many years have passed and I have not yet made the beginning.'

"We live in a different age, my father. I shall avoid thy mistakes.'

"Opportunity stands before thee, my son. It is offering a chance that may lead to wealth. I beg of thee, do not delay. Go upon the morrow to the son of my friend and bargain with him to pay ten percent of thy earnings into this investment. Go promptly upon the morrow. Opportunity waits for no man. Today it is here; soon it is gone. Therefore, delay not!'

"In spite of the advice of my father, I did hesitate. There were beautiful new robes just brought by the tradesmen from the East, robes of such richness and beauty my good wife and I felt we must each possess one. Should I agree to pay one-tenth of my earnings into the enterprise, we must deprive ourselves of these and other pleasures we dearly desired.

I delayed making a decision until it was too late, much to my subsequent regret. The enterprise did prove to be more profitable than any man had prophesied. This is my tale, showing how I did permit good luck to escape."

"In this tale we see how good luck waits to come to that man who accepts opportunity," commented a swarthy man of the desert. "To the building of an estate there must always be the beginning. That start may be a few pieces of gold or silver which a man diverts from his earnings to his first investment. I, myself, am the owner of many herds.

The start of my herds I did begin when I was a mere boy and did purchase with one piece of silver a young calf. This, being the beginning of my wealth, was of great importance to me.

"To take his first start to building an estate is as good luck as can come to any man. With all men, that first step, which changes them from men who earn from their own labor to men who draw dividends from the earnings of their gold, is important. Some, fortunately, take it when young and thereby outstrip in financial success those who do take it later or those unfortunate men, like the father of this merchant, who never take it.

"Had our friend, the merchant, taken this step in his early manhood when this opportunity came to him, this day he would be blessed with much more of this world's goods. Should the good luck of our friend, the cloth weaver, cause him to take such a step at this time, it will indeed be but the beginning of much greater good fortune."

"Thank you! I like to speak, also." A stranger from another country arose.

"I am a Syrian. Not so well do I speak your tongue. I wish to call this friend, the merchant, a name. Maybe you think it not polite, this name. Yet I wish to call him that. But, alas, I not know your word for it. If I do call it in Syrian, you will not understand. Therefore, please some good gentlemen, tell me that right name you call man who puts off doing those things that mighty good for him."

"Procrastinator," called a voice.

"That's him," shouted the Syrian, waving his hands excitedly, "he accepts not opportunity when she comes. He waits. He says I have much business right now. Bye and bye I talk to you. Opportunity, she will not wait for such slow fellow. She thinks if a man desires to be lucky he will step quick. Any man not step quick when opportunity comes, he big procrastinator like our friend, this merchant."

The merchant arose and bowed good naturedly in response to the laughter. "My admiration to thee, stranger within our gates, who hesitates not to speak the truth."

"And now let us hear another tale of opportunity. Who has for us another experience?" demanded Arkad.

"I have," responded a red-robed man of middle age. "I am a buyer of animals, mostly camels and horses. Sometimes I do also buy the sheep and goats. The tale I am about to relate will tell truthfully how opportunity came one night when I did least expect it. Perhaps for this reason I did let it escape. Of this you shall be the judge.

"Returning to the city one evening after a disheartening ten- days' journey in search of camels, I was much angered to find the gates of the city closed and locked. While my slaves spread our tent for the night, which we looked to spend with little food and no I water, I was approached by an elderly farmer who, like ourselves, found himself locked outside.

"Honored sir,' he addressed me, 'from thy appearance, I do judge thee to be a buyer. If this be so, much would I like to sell to thee the most excellent flock of sheep just driven up. Alas, my good wife lies very sick with the fever. I must return with all haste. Buy thou my sheep that I and my slaves may mount our camels and travel back without delay."

"So dark it was that I could not see his flock, but from the bleating I did know it must be large.

Having wasted ten days searching for camels I could not find, I was glad to bargain with him. In his anxiety, he did set a most reasonable price. I accepted, well knowing my slaves could drive the flock through the city gates in the morning and sell at a substantial profit.

The bargain concluded, I called my slaves to bring torches that we might count the flock which the farmer declared to contain nine hundred. I shall not burden you, my friends, with a description of our difficulty in attempting to count so many thirsty, restless, milling sheep. It proved to be an impossible task. Therefore, I bluntly informed the farmer I would count them at daylight and pay him then.

"Please, most honorable sir,' he pleaded, 'pay me but two-thirds of the price tonight that I may be on my way. I will leave my most intelligent and educated slave to assist to make the count in the morning. He is trustworthy and to him thou canst pay the balance.

"But I was stubborn and refused to make payment that night. Next morning, before I awoke, the city gates opened and four buyers rushed out in search of flocks. They were most eager and willing to pay high prices because the city was threatened with siege, and food was not plentiful. Nearly three times the price at which he had offered the flock to me did the old farmer receive for it. Thus was rare good luck allowed to escape."

"Here is a tale most unusual," commented Arkad. "What wisdom doth it suggest?"

"The wisdom of making a payment immediately when we are convinced our bargain is wise," suggested a venerable saddle maker. "If the bargain be good, then dost thou need protection against thy own weaknesses as much as against any other man. We mortals are changeable. Alas, I must say more apt to change our minds when right than wrong. Wrong, we are stubborn indeed. Right, we are prone to vacillate and let opportunity escape. My first judgment is my best.

Yet always have I found it difficult to compel myself to proceed with a good bargain when made. Therefore, as a protection against my own weaknesses, I do make a prompt deposit thereon. This doth save me from later regrets for the good luck that should have been mine."

"Thank you! Again I like to speak." The Syrian was upon his feet once more. "These tales much alike. Each time opportunity fly away for same reason. Each time she come to procrastinator, bringing good plan. Each time they hesitate, not say, right now best time, I do it quick. How can men succeed that way?"

"Wise are thy words, my friend," responded the buyer. "Good luck fled from procrastination in both these tales. Yet, this is not unusual. The spirit of procrastination is within all men. We desire riches; yet, how often when opportunity doth appear before us, that spirit of procrastination from within doth urge various delays in our acceptance.

In listening to it we do become our own worst enemies. "In my younger days I did not know it by this long word our friend from Syria doth enjoy. I did think at first it was my own poor judgment that did cause me loss of many profitable trades. Later, I did credit it to my stubborn disposition. At last, I did recognize it for what it was—a habit of needless delaying where action was required, action prompt and decisive.

How I did hate it when its true character stood revealed. With the bitterness of a wild ass hitched to a chariot, I did break loose from this enemy to my success."

"Thank you! I like ask question from Mr. Merchant." The Syrian was speaking.

"You wear fine robes, not like those of poor man. You speak like successful man. Tell us, do you listen now when procrastination whispers in your ear?"

"Like our friend the buyer, I also had to recognize and conquer procrastination," responded the merchant. "To me, it proved to be an enemy, ever watching and waiting to thwart my accomplishments.

The tale I did relate is but one of many similar instances I could tell to show how it drove away my opportunities. Tis not difficult to conquer, once understood. No man willingly permits the thief to rob his bins of grain. Nor does any man willingly permit an enemy to drive away his customers and rob him of his profits. When once I did recognize that such acts as these my enemy was committing, with determination I conquered him. So must every man master his own spirit of procrastination before he can expect to share in the rich treasures of Babylon.

"What sayest, Arkad? Because thou art the richest man in Babylon, many do proclaim thee to be the luckiest. Dost agree with me that no man can arrive at a full measure of success until he hath completely crushed the spirit of procrastination within him?"

"It is even as thou sayest," Arkad admitted. "During my long life I have watched generation following generation, marching forward along those avenues of trade, science and learning that lead to success in life.

Opportunities came to all these men. Some grasped theirs and moved steadily to the gratification of their deepest desires, but the majority hesitated, faltered and fell behind."

Arkad turned to the cloth weaver. Thou didst suggest that we debate good luck. Let us hear what thou now thinkest upon the subject."

"I do see good luck in a different light. I had thought of it as something most desirable that might happen to a man without effort upon his part.

Now, I do realize such happenings are not the sort of thing one may attract to himself.

From our discussion have I learned that to attract good luck to oneself, it is necessary to take advantage of opportunities. Therefore, in the future, I shall endeavor to make the best of such opportunities as do come to me."

"Thou hast well grasped the truths brought forth in our discussion," Arkad replied. "Good luck, we do find, often follows opportunity but seldom comes otherwise. Our merchant friend would have found great good luck had he accepted the opportunity the good goddess did present to him. Our friend the buyer, likewise, would have enjoyed good luck had he completed the purchase of the flock and sold at such a handsome profit.

"We did pursue this discussion to find a means by which good luck could be enticed to us. I feel that we have found the way. Both the tales did illustrate how good luck follows opportunity. Herein lies a truth that many similar tales of good luck, won or lost, could not change. The truth is this: Good luck can be enticed by accepting opportunity.

"Those eager to grasp opportunities for their betterment, do attract the interest of the good goddess. She is ever anxious to aid those who please her. Men of action please her best.

"Action will lead thee forward to the successes thou dost desire."

Men Of Action Are Favored By The Goddess Of Good Luck

SUMMARY
Guide

Arkad had his own special hall in the Temple of Learning where he expounded his teachings of wealth to anyone who desired to be rich.

One particular evening, a cloth weaver related his experience of picking up a gold purse, and he wanted to be always lucky like that, and the men started sharing their own stories.

In usual cases like trading businesses, the traders usually would reap profits if they persisted.

However, things became different at the wagers, where the odds favored the game keeper instead. Therefore while some people would win the wagers, most often than it, everyone suffered losses. In these scenarios where the odds don't favor the majority, winning was considered false luck.

A merchant offered his insights:

Many years ago, his father came to him, telling him of a piece of barren which was located high above a canal. The father had a idea to purchase the land, build large water wheels to collect the water to irrigate the soil. However both father and son were not rich, so they recruited a group of men who would deposit with the father and son a portion of their earnings. The idea was eventually implemented and it became profitable for them.

Another merchant, a trader in animals such as camels and horses, shared his story: One night, after he returned from a disheartening search for camels, he was dismayed to find that the city gates were already locked, so he and his slaves had to camp outside. A farmer, who was also locked out, approached him to sell his sheep.

They concluded their business easily, despite the merchant being unable to count the sheep because it was too dark. Although the farmer wanted a two-third payment, the merchant refused. The next morning, four buyers came out, saw his flock and approached him. Because the city was threatened with a siege, and that food was not plentiful, the buyers quickly settled at a price with the merchant - which was three times which the farmer asked for!

From the experiences, a saddle maker came up with a conclusion: Make the deal if the bargain looked good. In addition, a person had to recognize and conquer procrastination.

At the end of the sharing session, Arkad summarized the most important point of the discussion:

🏛   To attract good luck, one must be willing to take advantage of opportunities.

LEARNING / LESSON

The learning lesson here is about random and profitable luck.

Random luck refers to finding a sum of money on the ground, for instance.

Profitable luck refers to the opportunities that could be capitalized on to gain success or wealth.

A modern example comes from Luxe Valet (www.luxe.com).

It works like this: Drivers who need to park their vehicles where it is difficult to find a lot can access the Luxe app and indicate where they would like to park. When they arrive there, the valet will take over the car to park it while the driver continues on his or her way. When the driver wants the car back, he or she accesses the app again and indicate the location to bring the car to.

In fact, the car can also be washed or the tank filled up if the driver indicates so.

How does this relate to opportunity?

Well, the opportunity is based on demand and imbalance. Demand, because the drivers are unable to find the parking lots at the places they want to go to.

Imbalance, because there are carparks and garages that are not properly utilized!

So this is where Luxe Valet comes in. They effectively become the middleman, and liaise with the drivers and also the empty carparks and the garages.

This is effective because the problem is solved - cars get parked no matter where, and the carparks and garages are fully utilized all the time!

Here we look at 5 different ways to make your own opportunities, and luck!

🏛 **Use Your Optimism** - Optimistic people naturally make their own luck. According to research studies, more than 80% of people who think they are lucky actually work HARD at making their own, good, luck. Therefore, always see the world with a positive eye.

🏛 **Be Open-Minded** - Don't always think "No, that wouldn't work!" when you look at things. Keep your mind open and look at opportunities that can be potentially rewarding. Learn to evaluate with a critical-thinking mind.

🏛 **"If Only"** - Many a time people would always say, "If only I did that..." and rue the opportunities they let slipped. When your intuition, or inner voice, leans towards the opportunity, grab it!

🏛 **Shoot For The Moon** - Dream big and set your goals (realistically of course). Implement the strategies and action steps to work towards the goals.

🏛 **(No) Finish Line** - In life, there is essentially no finish line. Whether you are studying or working, always be open-minded and keep on learning new skills or knowledge. Be committed towards growth and positive thinking, and you will find that your opportunities are creating all the luck in the world - just for you!

THE FIVE LAWS OF GOLD

"A bag heavy with gold or a clay tablet carved with words of wisdom; if thou hadst thy choice, which wouldst thou choose?"

By the flickering light from the fire of desert shrubs, the sun-tanned faces of the listeners gleamed with interest.

"The gold, the gold," chorused the twenty-seven.

Old Kalabab smiled knowingly.

"Hark," he resumed, raising his hand. "Hear the wild dogs out there in the night. They howl and wail because they are lean with hunger. Yet feed them, and what do they? Fight and strut. Then fight and strut some more, giving no thought to the morrow that will surely come.

"Just so it is with the sons of men. Give them a choice of gold and wisdom— what do they do?

Ignore the wisdom and waste the gold. On the morrow they wail because they have no more gold.

"Gold is reserved for those who know its laws and abide by them."

Kalabab drew his white robe close about his lean legs, for a cool night wind was blowing.

"Because thou hast served me faithfully upon our long journey, because thou cared well for my camels, because thou toiled uncomplainingly across the hot sands of the desert, because thou fought bravely the robbers that sought to despoil my merchandise, I will tell thee this night the tale of the five laws of gold, such a tale as thou never hast heard before.

"Hark ye, with deep attention to the words I speak, for if you grasp their meaning and heed them, in the days that come thou shalt have much gold."

He paused impressively. Above in a canopy of blue, the stars shone brightly in the crystal clear skies of Babylonia. Behind the group loomed their faded tents tightly staked against possible desert storms. Beside the tents were neatly stacked bales of merchandise covered with skins. Nearby the camel herd sprawled in the sand, some chewing their cuds contentedly, others snoring in hoarse discord.

"Thou hast told us many good tales, Kalabab," spoke up the chief packer. "We look to thy wisdom to guide us upon the morrow when our service with thee shall be at an end."

"I have but told thee of my adventures in strange and distant lands, but this night I shall tell thee of the wisdom of Arkad, the wise rich man."

"Much have we heard of him," acknowledged the chief packer, "for he was the richest man that ever lived in Babylon."

"The richest man he was, and that because be was wise in the ways of gold, even as no man had ever been before him. This night shall I tell you of his great wisdom as it was told to me by Nomasir, his son, many years ago in Nineveh, when I was but a lad.

"My master and myself had tarried long into the night in the palace of Nomasir. I had helped my master bring great bundles of fine rugs, each one to be tried by Nomasir until his choice of colors was satisfied. At last he was well pleased and commanded us to sit with him and to drink a rare vintage odorous to the nostrils and most warming to my stomach, which was unaccustomed to such a drink.

"Then, did he tell us this tale of the great wisdom of Arkad, his father, even as I shall tell it to you.

"In Babylon it is the custom, as you know, that the sons of wealthy fathers live with their parents in expectation of inheriting the estate. Arkad did not approve of this custom. Therefore, when Nomasir reached man's estate, he sent for the young man and addressed him:

"My son, it is my desire that thou succeed to my estate. Thou must, however, first prove that thou art capable of wisely handling it. Therefore, I wish that thou go out into the world and show thy ability both to acquire gold and to make thyself respected among men.

"To start thee well, I will give thee two things of which I, myself, was denied when I started as a poor youth to build up a fortune.

"First, I give thee this bag of gold. If thou use it wisely, it will be the basis of thy future success.

"Second, I give thee this clay tablet upon which is carved the five laws of gold. If thou dost but interpret them in thy own acts, they shall bring thee competence and security.

"Ten years from this day come thou back to the house of thy father and give account of thyself. If thou prove worthy, I will then make thee the heir to my estate. Otherwise, I will give it to the priests that they may barter for my soul the land consideration of the gods.'
"So Nomasir went forth to make his own way, taking his bag of gold, the clay tablet carefully wrapped in silken cloth, his slave and the horses upon which they rode.

"The ten years passed, and Nomasir, as he had agreed, returned to the house of his father who provided a great feast in his honor, to which he invited many friends and relatives. After the feast was over, the father and mother mounted their throne-like seats at one side of the great hall, and Nomasir stood before them to give an account of himself as he had promised his father.

It was evening. The room was hazy with smoke from the wicks of the oil lamps that but dimly lighted it. Slaves in white woven jackets and tunics fanned the humid air rhythmically with long-stemmed palm leaves. A stately dignity colored the scene. The wife of Nomasir and his two young sons, with friends and other members of the family, sat upon rugs behind him, eager listeners.

"My father,' he began deferentially, I bow before thy wisdom. Ten years ago when I stood at the gates of manhood, thou bade me go forth and become a man among men, instead of remaining a vassal to thy fortune.

"Thou gave me liberally of thy gold. Thou gave me liberally of thy wisdom. Of the gold, alas!

I must admit of a disastrous handling. It fled, indeed, from my inexperienced hands even as a wild hare flees at the first opportunity from the youth who captures it.'

The father smiled indulgently. "Continue, my son, thy tale interests me in all its details."

"I decided to go to Nineveh, as it was a growing city, believing that I might find there opportunities. I joined a caravan and among its members made numerous friends. Two well-spoken men who had a most beautiful white horse as fleet as the wind were among these.

"As we journeyed, they told me in confidence that in Nineveh was a wealthy man who owned a horse so swift that it had never been beaten. Its owner believed that no horse living could run with greater speed. Therefore, would he wager any sum however large that his horse could outspeed any horse in all Babylonia. Compared to their horse, so my friends said, it was but a lumbering ass that could be beaten with ease.

"They offered, as a great favor, to permit me to join them in a wager. I was quite carried away with the plan.

"Our horse was badly beaten and I lost much of my gold.' The father laughed. 'Later, I discovered that this was a deceitful plan of these men and they constantly journeyed with caravans seeking victims. You see, the man in Nineveh was their partner and shared with them the bets he won.

This shrewd deceit taught me my first lesson in looking out for myself.

"I was soon to learn another, equally bitter. In the caravan was another young man with whom I became quite friendly. He was the son of wealthy parents and, like myself, journeying to Nineveh to find a suitable location.

Not long after our arrival, he told me that a merchant had died and his shop with its rich merchandise and patronage could be secured at a paltry price. Saying that we would be equal partners but first he must return to Babylon to secure his gold, he prevailed upon me to purchase the stock with my gold, agreeing that his would be used later to carry on our venture.

"He long delayed the trip to Babylon, proving in the meantime to be an unwise buyer and a foolish spender. I finally put him out, but not before the business had deteriorated to where we had only unsalable goods and no gold to buy other goods. I sacrificed what was left to an Israelite for a pitiful sum.

"Soon there followed, I tell you, my father, bitter days. I sought employment and found it not, for I was without trade or training that would enable me to
earn. I sold my horses. I sold my slave. I sold my extra robes that I might have food and a place to sleep, but each day grim want crouched closer.

"But in those bitter days, I remembered thy confidence in me, my father.

Thou hadst sent me forth to become a man, and this I was determined to accomplish.' The mother buried her face and wept softly. "At this time, I bethought me of the table thou had given to me upon which thou had carved the five laws of gold. Thereupon, I read most carefully thy words of wisdom, and realized that had I but sought wisdom first, my gold would not have been lost to me.

I learned by heart each law and determined that, when once more the goddess of good fortune smiled upon me, I would be guided by the wisdom of age and not by the inexperience of youth.

"For the benefit of you who are seated here this night, I will read the wisdom of my father as engraved upon the clay tablet which he gave to me ten years ago:

THE FIVE LAWS OF GOLD

i. Gold cometh gladly and in increasing quantity to any man who will put by not less than one-tenth of his earngs to create an estate for his future and that of his family.

ii. Gold laboreth diligently and contentedly for the wise owner who finds for it profitable employment, multiplying even as the flocks of the field.

iii. Gold clingeth to the protection of the cautious owner who invests it under the advice of men wise in its handling.

iv. Gold slippeth away from the man who invests it in businesses or purposes with which he is not familiar or which are not approved by those skilled in its keep.

v.   Gold flees the man who would force it to impossible earnings or who followeth the alluring advice of tricksters and schemers or who trusts it to his own inexperience and romantic desires in investment.

"These are the five laws of gold as written by my father. I do proclaim them as of greater value than gold itself, as I will show by the continuance of my tale.'

"He again faced his father. 'I have told thee of the depth of poverty and despair to which my inexperience brought me.

"However, there is no chain of disasters that will not come to an end. Mine came when I secured employment managing a crew of slaves working upon the new outer wall of the city. "

'Profiting from my knowledge of the first law of gold, I saved a copper from my first earnings, adding to it at every opportunity until I had a piece of silver. It was a slow procedure, for one must live.

I did spend grudgingly, I admit, because I was determined to earn back before the ten years were over as much gold as you, my father, had given to me.

"One day the slave master, with whom I had become quite friendly, said to me: "Thou art a thrifty youth who spends not wantonly what he earns. Hast thou gold put by that is not earning?" "

'Yes,' I replied, 'It is my greatest desire to accumulate gold to replace that which my father gave to me and which I have lost.'

"Tis a worthy ambition, I will grant, and do you know that the gold which you have saved can work for you and earn much more gold?"

"Alas! my experience has been bitter, for my father's gold has fled from me, and I am in much fear lest my own do the same.'

"If thou hast confidence in me, I will give thee a lesson in the profitable handling of gold," he replied. "Within a year the outer wall will be complete and ready for the great gates of bronze that will be built at each entrance to protect the city from the king's enemies.

In all Nineveh there is not enough metal to make these gates and the king has not thought to provide it. Here is my plan: A group of us will pool our gold and send a caravan to the mines of copper and tin, which are distant, and bring to Nineveh the metal for the gates.

When the king says, 'Make the great gates,' we alone can supply the metal and a rich price he will pay. If the king will not buy from us, we will yet have the metal which can be sold for a fair price."

"In his offer I recognized an opportunity to abide by the third law and invest my savings under the guidance of wise men. Nor was I disappointed. Our pool was a success, and my small store of gold was greatly increased by the transaction.

"In due time, I was accepted as a member of this same group in other ventures. They were men wise in the profitable handling of gold. They talked over each plan presented with great care, before entering upon it. They would take no chance on losing their principal or tying it up in unprofitable investments from which their gold could not be recovered.

Such foolish things as the horse race and the partnership into which I had entered with my inexperience would have had scant consideration with them. They would have immediately pointed out their weaknesses.

"Through my association with these men, I learned to safely invest gold to bring profitable returns. As the years went on, my treasure increased more and more rapidly. I not only made back as much as I lost, but much more.

"Through my misfortunes, my trials and my success, I have tested time and again the wisdom of the five laws of gold, my father, and have proven them true in every test. To him who is without knowledge of the five laws, gold comes not often, and goeth away quickly. But to him who abide by the five laws, gold comes and works as his dutiful slave.'

"Nomasir ceased speaking and motioned to a slave in the back of the room. The slave brought forward, one at a time, three heavy leather bags. One of these Nomasir took and placed upon the floor before his father addressing him again:

"Thou didst give to me a bag of gold, Babylon gold. Behold in its place, I do return to thee a bag of Nineveh gold of equal weight An equal exchange, as all will agree.

"Thou didst give to me a clay tablet inscribed with wisdom. Behold, in its stead, I do return two bags of gold.' So saying, he took from the slave the other two bags and, likewise, placed them upon the floor before his father.

"This I do to prove to thee, my father, of how much greater value I consider thy wisdom than thy gold. Yet, who can measure in bags of gold, the value of wisdom? Without wisdom, gold is quickly lost by those who have it, but with wisdom, gold can be secured by those who have it not, as these three bags of gold do prove.

"It does, indeed, give to me the deepest satisfaction, my father, to stand before thee and say that, because of thy wisdom, I have been able to become rich and respected before men.'

"The father placed his hand fondly upon the head of Nomasir. 'Thou hast learned well thy lessons, and I am, indeed, fortunate to have a son to whom I may entrust my wealth.'

" Kalabab ceased his tale and looked critically at his listeners.

"What means this to thee, this tale of Nomasir?" he continued.

"Who amongst thee can go to thy father or to the father of thy wife and give an account of wise handling of his earnings?

"What would these venerable men think were you to say: 'I have traveled much and learned much and labored much and earned much, yet alas, of gold I have little. Some I spent wisely, some I spent foolishly and much I lost in unwise ways.'

"Dost still think it but an inconsistency of fate that some men have much gold and others have naught? Then you err.

"Men have much gold when they know the five laws of gold and abide thereby.

"Because I learned these five laws in my youth and abided by them, I have become a wealthy merchant. Not by some strange magic did I accumulate my wealth.

"Wealth that comes quickly goeth the same way.

"Wealth that stayeth to give enjoyment and satisfaction to its owner comes gradually, because it is a child born of knowledge and persistent purpose.

"To earn wealth is but a slight burden upon the thoughtful man. Bearing the burden consistently from year to year accomplishes the final purpose.

"The five laws of gold offer to thee a rich reward for their observance. "Each of these five laws is rich with meaning and lest thou overlook this in the briefness of my tale, I will now repeat them. I do know them each by heart because in my youth, I could see their value and would not be content until I knew them word for word.

THE FIRST LAW OF GOLD

Gold cometh gladly and in increasing quantity to any man who will put by not less than one-tenth of his earnings to create an estate for his future and that of his family.

"Any man who will put by one-tenth of his earnings consistently and invest it wisely will surely create a valuable estate that will provide an income for him in the future and further guarantee safety for his family in case the gods call him to the world of darkness.

This law always sayeth that gold cometh gladly to such a man. I can truly certify this in my own life. The more gold I accumulate, the more readily it comes to me and in increased quantities. The gold which I save earns more, even as yours will, and its earnings earn more, and this is the working out of the first law."

THE SECOND LAW OF GOLD

Gold laboreth diligently and contentedly for the wise owner who finds for it profitable employment, multiplying even as the flocks of the field.

"Gold, indeed, is a willing worker. It is ever eager to multiply when opportunity presents itself. To every man who hath a store of gold set by, opportunity comes for its most profitable use. As the years pass, it multiplies itself in surprising fashion."

THE THIRD LAW OF GOLD

Gold clingeth to the protection of the cautious owner who invests it under the advice of men wise in its handling.

"Gold, indeed, clingeth to the cautious owner, even as it flees the careless owner. The man who seeks the advice of men wise in handling gold soon learneth not to jeopardize his treasure, but to preserve in safety and to enjoy in contentment its consistent increase."

THE FOURTH LAW OF GOLD

Gold slippeth away from the man who invests it in businesses or purposes with which he is not familiar or which are not approved by those skilled in its keep.

To the man who hath gold, yet is not skilled in its handling, many uses for it appear most profitable. Too often these are fraught with danger of loss, and if properly analyzed by wise men, show small possibility of profit.

Therefore, the inexperienced owner of gold who trusts to his own judgment and invests it in business or purposes with which he is not familiar, too often finds his judgment imperfect, and pays with his treasure for his inexperience. Wise, indeed is he who investeth his treasures under the advice of men skilled In the ways of gold."

THE FIFTH LAW OF GOLD

Gold flees the man who would force it to impossible earnings or who followeth the alluring advice of tricksters and schemers or who trusts it to his own inexperience and romantic desires in investment.

"Fanciful propositions that thrill like adventure tales always come to the new owner of gold. These appear to endow his treasure with magic powers that will enable it to make impossible earnings. Yet heed ye the wise men for verily they know the risks that lurk behind every plan to make great wealth suddenly.

"Forget not the rich men of Nineveh who would take no chance of losing their principal or tying it up in unprofitable investments. "This ends my tale of the five laws of gold. In telling it to thee, I have told the secrets of my own success.

"Yet, they are not secrets but truths which every man must first learn and then follow who wishes to step out of the multitude that, like you wild dogs, must worry each day for food to eat.

"Tomorrow, we enter Babylon. Look! See the fire that burns eternal above the Temple of Bel! We are already in sight of the golden city.

Tomorrow, each of thee shall have gold, the gold thou has so well earned by thy faithful services.

"Ten years from this night, what can you tell about this gold?

"If there be men among you, who, like Nomasir, will use a portion of their gold to start for themselves an estate and be thenceforth wisely guided by the wisdom of Arkad, ten years from now, 'tis a safe wager, like the son of Arkad, they will be rich and respected among men.

"Our wise acts accompany us through life to please us and to help us. Just as surely, our unwise acts follow us to plague and torment us.

Alas, they cannot be forgotten. In the front rank of the torments that do follow us are the memories of the things we should have done, of the opportunities which came to us and we took not.

"Rich are the treasures of Babylon, so rich no man can count their value in pieces of gold. Each year, they grow richer and more valuable. Like the treasures of every land, they are a reward, a rich reward awaiting those men of purpose who determine to secure their just share.

"In the strength of thine own desires is a magic power. Guide this power with thy knowledge of the five laws of gold and thou shall share the treasures of Babylon."

In this chapter, Kalabab, a trader, is travelling with the company of 27 men. He asks them, "If you had a choice, would you choose a bag filled with gold, or a clay tablet with words of wisdom carved on it?" As he predicted, the 27 men unanimously favored the gold over the unimpressive-sounding clay tablet. Kalabab decides to impart some wisdom to these men in the form of Arkad and Nomasir's story.

The natural order of things back then was that when a man died, his estate and all his assets would go to his heir. But Arkad didn't want to leave his estate to his son, Nomasir, without ensuring his son's competency in handling finances. So he set Nomasir on a journey into the world outside to make his own fortune, equipping him with a bag of gold and a clay tablet with words of wisdom on it, to return home only after ten years.

At the beginning, Nomasir ignored the clay tablet. Two men he befriended told him of a man in Nineveh who had a horse that had never been beaten in speed. Hence that man would bet any amount that his horse would win any race. These two men had a stunning white horse with them that they claimed could beat any horse with ease, and invited Nomasir to join in their wager.

Nomasir thought it was a quick way to get rich and agreed without much hesitation. Their horse was then defeated easily and Nomasir lost a huge chunk of his gold. Afterwards he found out that these two men and the man in Nineveh were in cahoots all along, scamming people out of their money.

Nomasir then became friends with another man who told him of a shop whose owner had passed away, and the shop could be purchased at a meager price, with all merchandise intact. The man proposed a partnership where both of them would be equal investors, but that he had to retrieve his gold from Babylon, so Nomasir had to fork out the gold for the shop and its wares first.

It turned out that the man was frivolous in his spending, and kept delaying the trip back to Babylon for his share of the gold. The business soon ran out of money and Nomasir had to sell it off for a miserable amount of money.

All these ventures cost him almost all of his gold and couldn't find a job because of his lack of skills and experience. He sold his horses, slave, and even his extra clothing just to survive.

Finally he remembered the clay tablet, and read it in desperation:

1. "Gold cometh gladly and in increasing quantity to any man who will put by not less than one-tenth of his earnings to create an estate for his future and that of his family."
   (Save 10% of your income to ensure a stable future)

2. "Gold laboreth diligently and contentedly for the wise owner who finds for it profitable employment, multiplying even as the flocks of the field."
   (Let your money work for you - term deposits, managed funds, real estate)

3. "Gold clingeth to the protection of the cautious owner who invests it under the advice of men wise in its handling."
   (Heed only trustworthy advice)

4. Gold slippeth away from the man who invests it in businesses or purposes with which he is not familiar or which are not approved by those skilled in its keep."
(Don't invest in anything you're not familiar with)

5. "Gold flees the man who would force it to impossible earnings or who followeth the alluring advice of tricksters and schemers or who trusts it to his own inexperience and romantic desires in investment."
(Stay away from deals that sound too good to be true)

Nomasir then realized his foolishness in his ventures, and became determined to earn back the gold he lost by following the five laws diligently. He found a job managing a crew of slaves who were working on the new outer wall of the city, and saved a copper (out of ten) from each of his earnings.

By doing this, he amassed a small sum of money. After observing that Nomasir was frugal with his finances, the slave master offered Nomasir an opportunity to invest in his project of obtaining metal from somewhere far and selling it to the king for a great profit (the king would need metal for the gates of the new outer wall, and the city had insufficient resources of metal).

As Nomasir had become friends with the slave master and trusted him, he recognized the chance to apply the third law of gold, and decided to invest under the guidance of this wise man. His gold then multiplied after being accepted into the slave master's circle of other wise men who were conscientious and smart about their money.

Ten years passed, and Nomasir returned home to his parents, and told his father everything that had happened. He then lay a bag of gold in front of his father, in return for the bag of gold Arkad gave to him ten years ago. And for the wisdom on the clay tablet, Nomasir offered two bags of gold. This was Nomasir's way of showing how he valued his father's wisdom more than the gold he'd given him. Arkad was pleased and thus bequeathed his wealth to his son without hesitation.

THE FIRST LAW OF GOLD

"Gold cometh gladly and in increasing quantity to any man who will put by not less than one-tenth of his earnings to create an estate for his future and that of his family."

What this essentially means: Save 10% of your income to ensure a stable future

#1: I've covered this before and I can't stress it enough: **start saving**.

It can be really difficult to save money for a rainy day, a future investment, that expensive item you covet - it's tough, period. Many people spend their monthly paycheck on bills, credit card debts, groceries, etc. But if you do this one thing before you start spending your hard-earned money, it makes a world of difference.

Earlier on, you realized that you need to save a tenth of your income. Make sure that you've deducted the tax dollars first. Before you even allocate any money to save or spend, be sure to pay your taxes first. Create a separate account for taxes if you have to.

Now, for example your income is $100 (after tax dollars). Take $10 and put it into a savings account different from the one you use for expenditures. This is important.

Don't keep your 10% savings in the same account as your spending account, because it's easy to be tempted at the end of the month when you're running a little tight, and you see that balance of 10% in there. You'll probably think, "Oh, it's just one time. I'll just use it first and make it up next month." Or worse, you don't even plan on making up the difference.

It might work for a month or two, but eventually you will slip right into spending 100% of your income. Be disciplined and gradually you will start to see the buildup of money in that savings account and feel compelled to make it grow faster.

Nomasir became rich because he diligently followed this first law of gold.

#2: Now, we've established that it's imperative to save 10% to fatten your purse. But what about the 90% left?

That's where you need to start budgeting. The common misconception is that budgeting means you have to scrimp and save and deny yourself the pleasures in life. But that's totally wrong.

Budgeting simply allows you to have a tighter rein on your spending, so that you can spend on the pleasures of life guilt-free. Why shouldn't you spend what you earned on things you like?

The main thing here is not to overspend. Even celebrities who have net worth of millions still lead a frugal life, like Keanu Reeves ($350 million) who still takes the subway, and Kristen Bell ($16 million), who "almost shops exclusively with coupons" and had a wedding that cost only $142.

So every month, before you start spending or even saving, allocate your paycheck properly so that you know where every cent goes, instead of spending on credit.

🏛 Step 1: Take a pen and paper - or create a fancy Excel spreadsheet if you prefer - and start allocating your paycheck to different uses.

- **10% Savings**

As I've mentioned earlier, if you already have many commitments or debts that exceed 90% of your income, then saving 1 or 2% is still fine - as long as you start the habit of saving.

The point is that these savings are meant as seed money/capital for investments, fiscal growth - not to be touched for purchases or active businesses. I'll cover more on this later in the second law.

- **55% Necessities**

55% goes to necessities such as bills, groceries, daily meals, transportation fees, car payments, study loans, and such.

Now, this is just a guideline, but it's been tried and tested with successful results, so if you're able to follow these percentages then all the better.

- **10% Long-Term Goals**

This allocation is for that vacation to Hawaii you always dreamed of, a nice Chanel wallet, a gold Rolex, your kids' college fund - whatever big expense you want. But only put 10% towards it because this is a long-term goal. You need to fit these goals into the big picture. Or else you'll be tempted to put more into these goals and end up with a Chanel bag and no money for groceries.

-
- **10% Education**

We should always strive to "upgrade" ourselves, just like how software needs version updates. In today's fast-paced society, we can't afford to let ourselves go and become complacent or younger, more competent people will rise up and you will be left in their dust.

Take classes that are helpful to your trade, or even pick up a new skill - you never know when it might come in handy.

- **10% Entertainment**

I didn't say you weren't allowed to have fun! This portion of your income is for you to splurge on yourself. Book a well-deserved massage, catch the latest blockbuster or buy yourself some fresh flowers to brighten up your desk.

Whatever it is, you've done all you needed to do for the month money-wise: there're no more bills or debts to pay, you've set aside savings both for fiscal growth and for long-term goals and etc. What's left is for you to indulge yourself and enjoy life as it is. Why work so hard if you can't unwind and relax for a bit?

- **5% Charity/Allocate to Savings or Long-Term Goals**

    Some people are used to giving 10% (such as tithing), which you can certainly do, but take the 5% from necessities instead of the other categories.

    It's always good to lower your necessities because that means you are saving money from unnecessary expenses - perhaps by taking the bus more often or switching from brand name products to generic ones.

    It's better to lower your necessities' percentage than your entertainment's because you derive more satisfaction from entertainment, which will give you more incentive and motivation to stick to your budget. If you take 5% off it instead of necessities, you might feel like it's hard to follow through because you're not getting any (instant) gratification out of it.

🏛 **Step 2**: Divide your paycheck into different accounts as allocated above. Use checking accounts or those with ATM cards for your necessities, education, and entertainment. As for your Savings or Long-Term Goals, look through multiple banks and see which one offers the highest interest rates and reasonable costs (you don't want to end up paying more in bank charges than your interest accrued!).

🏛 **Step 3**: Track your spending by keeping receipts and tallying your expenses at the end of the month.

Soon you'll begin to see a pattern of how you're spending your money and you can adjust your percentages more accurately. If you find that too exhausting, there are numerous websites that can help you keep your expenditures organized after you input the data.

THE SECOND LAW OF GOLD

"Gold laboreth diligently and contentedly for the wise owner who finds for it profitable employment, multiplying even as the flocks of the field."

What this essentially means: Let your money work for you - term deposits, managed funds, real estate, etc

Your money is the best kind of employee there is. It won't complain, it won't need any sick days, and won't throw any tantrums. It will just work ceaselessly as long as you give it a job to do.

Most of us with savings in our accounts don't usually employ them well. We allow the money to sit in there, stagnant, accruing minimal interest over the years. Even if some banks offer higher interest rates, those amounts are nothing compared to the amount you can get if you invest your money well.

When Nomasir accumulated enough gold, he didn't let the gold stay untouched. Under wise counsel, he invested in several projects that brought him high returns and multiplied his gold over time.

So you can follow suit and use your savings to earn extra income. But do take note that you should invest in passive income instead of active income.

Active income means that you have to put in some kind of effort for it. It could be opening a restaurant or clothing store, where you have to hire staff and buy inventory and pay for advertising, etc. That's a job.

What you should aim for is passive income, such as renting out properties or owning people's mortgages.

What Nomasir did was earn passive income where he put in gold and the slave master handled all of the minute details like hiring a caravan of workers to retrieve copper and tin for the gates.

Employing your money is not a slipshod decision, though. Some might go, "If I invest in designer purses or collectible figurines I may get rich in the future!" But that will take at least decades before the value of the item goes up, and sometimes it may even depreciate.

You'd think that high-salaried people like NFL players would be better off than us, but Sports Illustrated found that a whopping 78% of NFL players declare bankruptcy only two years after retirement! For NBA players, it's almost the same story: 60% of them are broke within 5 years.

Even the rich can make poor financial decisions and because of the sheer amount of money involved, their fall is even more devastating than the average person.

When probed further, we discover that most of these pro athletes' lack of financial stability are due to their lavish spending. NBA's Antoine Walker got arrested for writing bad checks to several casinos in 2009.

Judging from his $110 million career, this may sound ridiculous, but dig deeper and you'll realize that he didn't have the money to back his gambling debt because he had spent it all on luxury, customized cars such as Mercedes, Bentleys, and Cadillacs.

Instead of investing his money wisely, Walker fed his material desires and ended up broke and facing court charges.Therefore, you mustn't fall into the trap of spending exorbitantly and instead should secure your future (and your family's) by putting your money to work wisely.

🏛 **Step 1**: Put your money in a term deposit, which is the safest option there is. A term deposit is essentially a fixed-deposit account where you accrue a higher rate of interest than the usual savings accounts, but also requires a higher minimum deposit amount. Some banks can go as low as $1,000, but if you have more than that, it's good to put the bulk of it inside for safekeeping. The average interest rate is approximately 0.5% to 1%, which doesn't seem like much, but it's definitely better than letting your money sit and collect the dust of 0.03% (the standard rate of typical savings accounts)!

🏛 **Step 2**: Invest in managed funds. If you're not happy with the idea of keeping your money in a safe but slow-growing term deposit, you can try your hand at investing in managed funds. A managed fund is an investment portfolio that is managed by professional fund managers. You buy units. Your money is pooled together with other investors and the managers select a variety of investment funds for you. This is good for beginners as you can borrow the expertise of experts and have them do the grunt work for you. Also, managed funds are a good way to diversify your financial portfolio, and you can start investing with as little as $1,000. Find a reliable expert whom your close friends or family members have worked with before.

🏛 **Step 3**: If you have more capital on your hand, give passive businesses a go. Buying a Laundromat, parking lots, mortgage notes, rental property, etc. are good ways to earn passive income. Even investing in a Registered Retirement Savings Plan (RRSP) or an Individual Retirement Account (IRA) can be a good way to start. These two latter choices can give you some tax-free growth on your money. But be sure to consult someone who's familiar with these before you commit into anything!

THE THIRD LAW OF GOLD

"Gold clingeth to the protection of the cautious owner who invests it under the advice of men wise in its handling."

What this essentially means: Heed only trustworthy advice

How many times have you stretched your wallet too thin by buying some newfangled equipment recommended by a persuasive salesperson, then left whatever it was to become part of your decor and collect dust? Why is that? It's because you trusted the wrong person. The salesperson is just that: a person who wants to make a sale.

Sometimes even our friends may not have the best interests for us. Perhaps they get a commission, or a favor out of it, so they cajole you to join in on a new venture with them, or buy into some membership that you're never going to use. These are all wasted dollars.

Nomasir lost much of his gold when he trusted the two men he just met on a caravan. What did he know about them? Nothing, except that they were charming and spoke with confidence about their plan.

In Nineveh, note that the slave master didn't approach Nomasir to invest in his project right from the start. The slave master observed Nomasir for a period of time, assessing his sense of responsibility and abilities before he told him about his plan to sell metal to the king. Since they had both observed each other's financial habits, they could then decide to go into business together and earn a profit.

It is crucial to have someone that can keep your head level and teach you how to properly manage your finances without holding any punches. Financial advisors of celebrities often carry the difficult task of saying no to those who aren't used to hearing that word.

Margaret Black-Scott, an advisor based in Beverly Hills, shared about a famous boxer who wanted to withdraw $2 million in cash, but when was told the banks didn't have the cash on hand immediately, he threatened to throw his advisor out the window. A well-known business manager, Alan Reback, says that when a client wants to buy something extravagant like a Lamborghini, he counters it with a top-of-the-line BMW instead that makes more economic sense.

Be wary of people who go along with your every whim and fancy - perhaps they're just in it for the sweet ride or free treats. Instead, surround yourself with those who use logic to challenge your demands, those that make you realize how ridiculous it is to splurge on a designer item when your hands are still pretty tied financially. You'll find out who your true friends are: the ones who keep urging you to spend more on nice things, or those who are actually concerned about your financial future?

🏛 Stop succumbing to those who keep badgering you to join things like gym memberships. A run in the park is free, and works just as effectively. If you really need exercise equipment, find an inexpensive local community gym instead of those high-end ones.

🏛 Before you invest any money (following the Second Law of Gold), make sure the person you're working with is someone you trust. If he or she came from a friend or family's recommendation, ask that friend or family member why they trust him or her.

🏛 Listen carefully and read through every detail of any investment plan pitched to you. It's always good to get a second opinion where financial matters are involved. Do some research yourself if you can. Ask about potential risks and worst-case scenarios so that you won't be blindsided.

The Fourth Law Of Gold

"Gold slippeth away from the man who invests it in businesses or purposes with which he is not familiar or which are not approved by those skilled in its keep."

What this essentially means: Don't invest in anything you're not familiar with.

When Nomasir went into business with a man he barely knew, it fell apart shortly after he realized the man was not a good business partner. But by then it had been too late; Nomasir had suffered a huge loss.

This happens to many people who jump at the chance to make a profit, without acquiring more knowledge on the industry or market, without asking for second or even third opinions, without finding out more about the person they're going into business with.

And it's not just the average Joe who does this. Celebrities, with all their millions of dollars and worldwide fame, sometimes make the worst financial decisions. Britney Spears tried to start a Cajun restaurant called Nyla back in 2002, but she was young and had no experience in the business.

The restaurant closed in less than six months of operation. Jennifer Lopez, Eva Longoria, Hulk Hogan, Flava Flav all have tried their hand in the restaurant business but due to lack of knowledge and experience, failed miserably.

Nicky Hilton attempted to start her own chain of hotels, but despite her family name (Hilton Hotels), she just couldn't cut it and her project fell through just one year later. Nomasir was Arkad's son, but his lineage still could not have helped him achieve success had he not took his father's wisdom and worked hard.

🏛 Do thorough research on a subject that is new to you. Don't rely solely on others' advice. Even if the person is someone you trust, unforeseen circumstances may arise over the duration of the business or project, so it is always good for you to stay on top of things. Scores of people - including celebrities - have entrusted their entire fiscal responsibility to their advisors and managers, and ended up losing money. Sting, Billy Joel, and Rihanna are just a few examples of celebrities who were cheated by their trusted advisors.

THE FIFTH LAW OF GOLD

"Gold flees the man who would force it to impossible earnings or who followeth the alluring advice of tricksters and schemers or who trusts it to his own inexperience and romantic desires in investment."

What this essentially means: Stay away from deals that sound too good to be true

The largest Ponzi scheme in history can be attributed to Bernie Madoff, who blindsided every victim of his. The massive amount of $65 billion he scammed from his clients came from an exhaustive list of celebrity names: Kevin Bacon and his wife Kyra Sedgwick, Steven Spielberg, Larry King, John Malkovich, John Denver, along with countless big corporate organizations.

A Ponzi scheme often sounds too good to be true. But we can get so caught up in our fantasies of being rich (or richer, in celebrities' cases) that we momentarily forget to calculate the risks for ourselves, instead taking the word of someone with a glib tongue and a long list of big-name clients.

Celebrities are human, too. So it's perfectly understandable that they can make foolhardy choices sometimes; that's why almost all of them have finance managers or advisors.

However, some learnt the hard way on why it's prudent to find one that is trustworthy and reliable. In 2010, Kenneth Starr was arrested for defrauding a multitude of celebrities.

His mind-bogglingly extensive client list included Uma Thurman, Sylvester Stallone, Al Pacino, Diane Sawyer, Paul Simon, Liam Neeson, and that's just the tip of the iceberg!

They didn't know much about him, too, except that he was the accountant for yet another famous connection. According to one of his clients, his approach was to lay on the charm and tell his clients to buy whatever they want, that they could "afford it," lulling them into a false sense of security.

Then he persuaded them to give him their money for "investments." By the time the FBI caught up with him, it was too late; most of their money was never recovered.

This law brings to mind again how Nomasir trusted the two men from the caravan without thinking clearly of his risks, but focusing on his potential winnings despite knowing nothing about these men and their supposedly fast horse.

Anyone with a clear head would have asked for a demonstration of the horse's speed before agreeing to a bet with gold involved.

Gambling, high-risk investments, and unpredictable stocks are all quick ways to get rich - and also very quick ways to ending up broke. Unless you're clairvoyant, almost none of these will bring a return on your investments.

It's foolish to invest with instant huge profits in mind, because disappointment and heartache will be in the cards for you.

It may work out well once or twice for a few people, but a majority get their hands burnt in the stock market or through gambling, and end up destitute or estranged from loved ones.

🏛 Don't be blinded by greed. Greed is often the reason why people fall into get-rich-quick schemes and watch their money go up in flames. Nomasir tried to multiply his gold quickly and failed, but after he decided to find proper employment and earn his gold back, opportunities to multiply his gold found him instead. Patience is indeed a virtue that Nomasir has acquired.

🏛 Don't be hasty. Slow and steady often wins the race. For example, instead of risking your funds in high-risk, volatile day-trading (which involves sitting at your computer and watching the stock market continuously for the smallest bit of change), start small in managed funds. It's relatively low-risk, doesn't require your perpetual attention, and brings slow, steady returns over time.

THE GOLD LENDER OF BABYLON

Fifty pieces of gold! Never before had Rodan, the spearmaker of old Babylon, carried so much gold in his leather wallet. Happily down the king's highway from the palace of his most liberal Majesty he strode. Cheerfully the gold clinked as the wallet at his belt swayed with each step—the sweetest music he had ever heard.

Fifty pieces of gold! All his! He could hardly realize his good fortune. What power in those clinking discs! They could purchase anything he wanted, a grand house, land, cattle, camels, horses, chariots, whatever he might desire.

What use should he make of it? This evening as he turned into a side street towards the home of his sister, he could think of nothing he would rather possess than those same glittering, heavy pieces of gold—his to keep.

It was upon an evening some days later that a perplexed Rodan entered the shop of Mathon, the lender of gold and dealer in jewels and rare fabrics. Glancing neither to the right nor the left at the colorful articles artfully displayed, he passed through to the living quarters at the rear. Here he found the genteel Mathon lounging upon a rug partaking of a meal served by a black slave.

"I would counsel with thee for I know not what to do."

Rodan stood stolidly, feet apart, hairy breast exposed by the gaping front of his leather jacket. Mathon's narrow, sallow face smiled a friendly greeting. "What indiscretions hast thou done that thou shouldst seek the lender of gold? Hast been unlucky at the gaming table? Or hath some plump dame entangled thee? For many years have I known thee, yet never hast thou sought me to aid thee in thy troubles."

"No, no. Not such as that. I seek no gold. Instead I crave thy wise advice."

"Hear! Hear! What this man doth say. No one comes to the lender of gold for advice. My ears must play me false."

"They listen true."

"Can this be so? Rodan, the spearmaker, doth display more cunning than all the rest, for he comes to Mathon, not for gold, but for advice. Many men come to me for gold to pay for their follies, but as for advice, they want it not. Yet who is more able to advise than the lender of gold to whom many men come in trouble?

"Thou shalt eat with me, Rodan," he continued. Thou shalt be my guest for the evening. Andol" he commanded of the black slave, "draw up a rag for my friend, Rodan, the spearmaker, who comes for advice. He shall be mine honored guest. Bring to him much food and get for him my largest cup.

Choose well of the best wine that he may have satisfaction in the drinking. "Now, tell me what troubles thee."

"It is the king's gift."

"The king's gift? The king did make thee a gift and it gives thee trouble? What manner of gift?"

"Because he was much pleased with the design I did submit to him for a new point on the spears of the royal guard, he did present me with fifty pieces of gold, and now I am much perplexed.

"I am beseeched each hour the sun doth travel across the sky by those who would share it with me."

"That is natural. More men want gold than have it, and would wish one who comes by it easily to divide. But can you not say "No?" Is thy will not as strong as thy fist?"

"To many I can say no, yet sometimes it would be easier to say yes. Can one refuse to share with one's sister to whom he is deeply devoted?"

"Surely, thy own sister would not wish to deprive thee of enjoying thy reward."

"But it is for the sake of Araman, her husband, whom she wishes to see a rich merchant. She does feel that he has never had a chance and she beseeches me to loan to him this gold that he may become a prosperous merchant and repay me from his profits."

"My friend," resumed Mathon, "tis a worthy subject thou bringest to discuss. Gold bringeth unto its possessor responsibility and a changed position with his fellow men. It bringeth fear lest he lose it or it be tricked away from him. It bringeth a feeling of power and ability to do good. Likewise, it bringeth opportunities whereby his very good intentions may bring him into difficulties."

"Didst ever hear of the farmer of Nineveh who could understand the language of animals? I wot not, for 'tis not the kind of tale men like to tell over the bronze caster's forge. I will tell it to thee for thou shouldst know that to borrowing and lending there is more than the passing of gold from the hands of one to the hands of another.

"This farmer, who could understand what the animals said to each other, did linger in the farm yard each evening just to listen to their words. One evening he did hear the ox bemoaning to the ass the hardness of his lot: 'I do labor pulling the plow from morning until night.

No matter how hot the day, or how tired my legs, or how the bow doth chafe my neck, still must I work. But you are a creature of leisure.

You are trapped with a colorful blanket and do nothing more than carry our master about where he wishes to go. When he goes nowhere you do rest and eat the green grass all the day.'

"Now the ass, in spite of his vicious heels, was a goodly fellow and sympathized with the ox.

'My good friend, he replied, 'you do work very hard and I would help ease your lot. Therefore, will I tell you how you may have a day of rest. In the morning when the slave comes to fetch you to the plow, lie upon the ground and bellow much that he may say you are sick and cannot work.'

"So the ox took the advice of the ass and the next morning the slave returned to the farmer and told him the ox was sick and could not pull the plow.

"Then,' said the farmer, "hitch the ass to the plow for the plowing must go on.'

"All that day the ass, who had only intended to help his friend, found himself compelled to do the ox's task. When night came and he was released from the plow his heart was bitter and his legs were weary and his neck was sore where the bow had chafed it.

"The farmer lingered in the barnyard to listen.

"The ox began first. 'You are my good friend. Because of your wise advice I have enjoyed a day of rest.'

"And I,' retorted the ass, 'am like many another simple-hearted one who starts to help a friend and ends up by doing his task for him. Hereafter you draw your own plow, for I did hear the master tell the slave to send for the butcher were you sick again. I wish he would, for you are a lazy fellow.'

Thereafter they spoke to each other no more— this ended their friendship. Canst thou tell the moral to this tale, Rodan?"

"Tis a good tale," responded Rodan, "but I see not the moral."

"I thought not that you would. But it is there and simple too. Just this: If you desire to help thy friend, do so in a way that will not bring thy friend's burdens upon thyself."

"I had not thought of that. It is a wise moral. I wish not to assume the burdens of my sister's husband. But tell me. You lend to many. Do not the borrowers repay?"

Mathon smiled the smile of one whose soul is rich with much experience.

"Could a loan be well made if the borrower cannot repay? Must not the lender be wise and judge carefully whether his gold can perform a useful purpose to the borrower and return to him once more; or whether it will be wasted by one unable to use it wisely and leave him without his treasure, and leave the borrower with a debt he cannot repay? I will show to thee the tokens in my token chest and let them tell thee some of their stories."

Into the room he brought a chest as long as his arm covered with red pigskin and ornamented with bronze designs. He placed it upon the floor and squatted before it, both hands upon the lid.

"From each person to whom I lend, I do exact a token for my token chest, to remain there until the loan is repaid. When they repay I give back, but if they never repay it will always remind me of one who was not faithful to my confidence.

"The safest loans, my token box tells me, are to those whose possessions are of more value than the one they desire. They own lands, or jewels, or camels, or other things which could be sold to repay the loan.

Some of the tokens given to me are jewels of more value than the loan. Others are promises that if the loan be not repaid as agreed they will deliver to me certain property settlement. On loans like those I am assured that my gold will be returned with the rental thereon, for the loan is based on property.

"In another class are those who have the capacity to earn. They are such as you, who labor or serve and are paid. They have income and if they are honest and suffer no misfortune, I know that they also can repay the gold I loan them and the rental to which I am entitled. Such loans are based on human effort.

"Others are those who have neither property nor assured earning capacity. Life is hard and there will always be some who cannot adjust themselves to it. Alas for the loans I make them, even though they be no larger than a pence, my token box may censure me in the years to come unless they be guaranteed by good friends of the borrower who know him honorable."

Mathon released the clasp and opened the lid. Rodan leaned forward eagerly. At the top of the chest a bronze neck-piece lay upon a scarlet cloth.

Mathon picked up the piece and patted it affectionately. "This shall always remain in my token chest because the owner has passed on into the great darkness. I treasure, it, his token, and I treasure his memory; for he was my good friend. We traded together with much success until out of the east he brought a woman to wed, beautiful, but not like our women. A dazzling creature. He spent his gold lavishly to gratify her desires.

He came to me in distress when his gold was gone. I counseled with him. I told him I would help him to once more master his own affairs. He swore by the sign of the Great Bull that he would. But it was not to be. In a quarrel she thrust a knife into the heart he dared her to pierce."

"And she?" questioned Rodan.

"Yes, of course, this was hers." He picked up the scarlet cloth. "In bitter remorse she threw herself into the Euphrates. These two loans will never be repaid. The chest tells you, Rodan, that humans in the throes of great emotions are not safe risks for the gold lender.

"Here! Now this is different." He reached for a ring carved of ox bone. "This belongs to a farmer. I buy the rugs of his women. The locusts came and they had not food. I helped him and when the new crop came he repaid me. Later he came again and told of strange goats in a distant land as described by a traveler. They had long hair so fine and soft it would weave into rugs more beautiful than any ever seen in Babylon. He wanted a herd but he had no money. So I did lend him gold to make the journey and bring back goats.

Now his herd is begun and next year I shall surprise the lords of Babylon with the most expensive rugs it has been their good fortune to buy. Soon I must return his ring.

He doth insist on repaying promptly."

"Some borrowers do that?' queried Rodan.

"If they borrow for purposes that bring money back to them, I find it so. But if they borrow because of their indiscretions, I warn thee to be cautious if thou wouldst ever have thy gold back in hand again."

"Tell me about this," requested Rodan, picking up a heavy gold bracelet inset with jewels in rare designs.

"The women do appeal to my good friend," bantered Mathon.

"I am still much younger than you," retorted Rodan.

"I grant that, but this time thou doth suspicion romance where it is not. The owner of this is fat and wrinkled and doth talk so much and say so little she drives me mad. Once they had much money and were good customers, but ill times came upon them.

She has a son of whom she would make a merchant. So she came to me and borrowed gold that he might become a partner of a caravan owner who travels with his camels bartering in one city what he buys in another.

"This man proved a rascal for he left the poor boy in a distant city without money and without friends, pulling out early while the youth slept. Perhaps when this youth has grown to manhood, he will repay; until then I get no rental for the loan—only much talk. But I do admit the jewels are worthy of the loan."

"Did this lady ask thy advice as to the wisdom of the loan?"

"Quite otherwise. She had pictured to herself this son of hers as a wealthy and powerful man of Babylon. To suggest the contrary was to infuriate her. A fair rebuke I had. I knew the risk for this inexperienced boy, but as she offered security I could not refuse her.

"This," continued Mathon, waving a bit of pack rope tied into a knot, "belongs to Nebatur, the camel trader. When he would buy a herd larger than his funds he brings to me this knot and I lend to him according to his needs. He is a wise trader. I have confidence in his good judgment and can lend him freely. Many other merchants of Babylon have my confidence because of their honorable behavior.

Their 92tokens come and go frequently in my token box. Good merchants are an asset to our city and it profits me to aid them to keep trade moving that Babylon be prosperous."

Mathon picked out a beetle carved in turquoise and tossed it contemptuously on the floor. "A bug from Egypt. The lad who owns this does not care whether I ever receive back my gold. When I reproach him he replies, 'How can I repay when ill fate pursues me? You have plenty more.' What can I do? The token is his father's—a worthy man of small means who did pledge his land and herd to back his son's enterprises. The youth found success at first and then was over-zealous to gain great wealth.

His knowledge was immature. His enterprises collapsed. "Youth is ambitious. Youth would take short cuts to wealth and the desirable things for which it stands. To secure wealth quickly youth often borrows unwisely.

Youth, never having had experience, cannot realize that hopeless debt is like a deep pit into which one may descend quickly and where one may struggle vainly for many days. It is a pit of sorrow and regrets where the brightness of the sun is overcast and night is made unhappy by restless sleeping.

Yet, I do not discourage borrowing gold. I encourage it. I recommend it if it be for a wise purpose. I myself made my first real success as a merchant with borrowed gold.
"Yet, what should the lender do in such a case? The youth is in despair and accomplishes nothing. He is discouraged. He makes no effort to repay. My heart turns against depriving the father of his land and cattle."

"You tell me much that I am interested to hear," ventured Rodan, "but, I hear no answer to my question. Should I lend my fifty pieces of gold to my sister's husband? They mean much to me."

"Thy sister is a sterling woman whom I do much esteem. Should her husband come to me and ask to borrow fifty pieces of gold I should ask him for what purpose he would use it.

"If he answered that he desired to become a merchant like myself and deal in jewels and rich furnishings. I would say, 'What knowledge have you of the ways of trade? Do you know where you can buy at lowest cost? Do you know where you can sell at a fair price?" Could he say 'Yes' to these questions?"

"No, he could not," Rodan admitted. "He has helped me much in making spears and he has helped some in the shops."

"Then, would I say to him that his purpose was not wise. Merchants must learn their trade. His ambition, though worthy, is not practical and I would not lend him any gold.

"But, supposing he could say: 'Yes, I have helped merchants much. I know how to travel to Smyrna and to buy at low cost the rugs the housewives weave. I also know many of the rich people of Babylon to whom I can sell these at a large profit.' Then I would say: 'Your purpose is wise and your ambition honorable. I shall be glad to lend you the fifty pieces of gold if you can give me security that they will be returned."

But would he say, 'I have no security other than that I am an honored man and will pay you well for the loan.' Then would I reply, 'I treasure much each piece of gold. Were the robbers to take it from you as you journeyed to Smyrna or take the rugs from you as you returned, then you would have no means of repaying me and my gold would be gone.'

"Gold, you see, Rodan, is the merchandise of the lender of money. It is easy to lend. If it is lent unwisely then it is 94difficult to get back. The wise lender wishes not the risk of the undertaking but the guarantee of safe repayment. 'Tis well," he continued, "to assist those that are in trouble, 'tis well to help those upon whom fate has laid a heavy hand. 'Tis well to help those who are starting that they may progress and become valuable citizens. But help must be given wisely, lest, like the farmer's ass, in our desire to help we but take upon ourselves the burden that belongs to another.

"Again I wandered from thy question, Rodan, but hear my answer: Keep thy fifty pieces of gold. What thy labor earns for thee and what is given thee for reward is thine own and no man can put an obligation upon thee to part with it unless it do be thy wish. If thee wouldst lend it so that it may earn thee more gold, then lend with caution and in many places. I like not idle gold, even less I like too much of risk.

"How many years hast thou labored as a spearmaker?"

"Fully three." "How much besides the King's gift hast saved?"

"Three gold pieces."

"Each year that thou hast labored thou has denied thyself good things to save from thine earnings one piece of gold?"

"'Tis as you say."

"Then mightest save in fifty years of labor fifty pieces of gold by thy self-denial?"

"A lifetime of labor it would be."

"Thinkest thou thy sister would wish to jeopardize the savings of fifty years of labor over the bronze melting pot that her husband might experiment on being a merchant?"

"Not if I spoke in your words."

"Then go to her and say: 'Three years I have labored each day except fast days, from morning until night, and I have denied myself many things that my heart craved. For each year of labor and self-denial I have to show one piece of gold. Thou art my favored sister and I wish that thy husband may engage in business in which he will prosper greatly.

If he will submit to me a plan that seems wise and possible to my friend, Mathon, then will I gladly lend to him my savings of an entire year that he may have an opportunity to prove that he can succeed.' Do that, I say, and if he has within him the soul to succeed he can prove it. If he fails he will not owe thee more than he can hope some day to repay.

"I am a gold lender because I own more gold than I can use in my own trade. I desire my surplus gold to labor for others and thereby earn more gold. I do not wish to take risk of losing my gold for I have labored much and denied myself much to secure it. Therefore, I will no longer lend any of it where I am not confident that it is safe and will be returned to me. Neither will I lend it where I am not convinced that its earnings will be promptly paid to me.

"I have told to thee, Rodan, a few of the secrets of my token chest. From them you may understand the weakness of men and their eagerness to borrow that which they have no certain means to repay.
From this you can see how often their high hopes of the great earnings they could make, if they but had gold, are but false hopes they have not the ability or training to fulfill.

"Thou, Rodan, now have gold which thou shouldst put to earning more gold for thee. Thou art about to become even as I, a gold lender. If thou dost safely preserve thy treasure it will produce liberal earnings for thee and be a rich source of pleasure and profit during all thy days. But if thou dost let it escape from thee, it will be a source of constant sorrow and regret as long as thy memory doth last.

"What desirest thou most of this gold in thy wallet?"

"To keep it safe."

"Wisely spoken," replied Mathon approvingly. "Thy first desire is for safety. Thinkest thou that in the custody of thy sister's husband it would be truly safe from possible loss?"

"I fear not, for he is not wise in guarding gold."

"Then be not swayed by foolish sentiments of obligation to trust thy treasure to any person. If thou wouldst help thy family or thy friends, find other ways than risking the loss of thy treasure. Forget not that gold slippeth away in unexpected ways from those unskilled in guarding it. As well waste thy treasure in extravagance as let others lose it for thee.

"What next after safety dost desire of this treasure of thine?"

"That it earn more gold."

"Again thou speakest with wisdom. It should be made to earn and grow larger.

Gold wisely lent may even double itself with its earnings before a man like you groweth old. If you risk losing it you risk losing all that it would earn as well.

"Therefore, be not swayed by the fantastic plans of impractical men who think they see ways to force thy gold to make earnings unusually large. Such plans are the creations of dreamers unskilled in the safe and dependable laws of trade.

Be conservative in what thou expect it to earn that thou mayest keep and enjoy thy treasure. To hire it out with a promise of usurious returns is to invite loss.

"Seek to associate thyself with men and enterprises whose success is established that thy treasure may earn liberally under their skillful use and be guarded safely by their wisdom and experience.

"Thus, mayest thou avoid the misfortunes that follow most of the sons of men to whom the gods see fit to entrust gold."

When Rodan would thank him for his wise advice he would not listen, saying, "The king's gift shall teach thee much wisdom. If wouldst keep thy fifty pieces of gold thou must be discreet indeed.

Many uses will tempt thee. Much advice will be spoken to thee. Numerous opportunities to make large profits will be offered thee. The stories from my token box should warn thee, before thou let any piece of gold leave thy pouch to be sure that thou hast a safe way to pull it back again. Should my further advice appeal to thee, return again. It is gladly given.

"E're thou goest read this which I have carved beneath the lid of my token box. It applies equally to the borrower and the lender:

SUMMARY Guide

Rodan the spearmaker has just been given fifty pieces of gold by the king as a reward for his new spearhead design. Not entirely sure what he should do with his sudden windfall, Rodan goes to the gold lender of Babylon, Mathon, for advice. He tells Mathon that everyone around him is clamoring for a piece of his wealth, and he finds it especially hard to say no to his beloved sister.

Her husband is looking to start his own business and become a merchant, but needs Rodan's gold as capital.

Mathon tells him of a farmer in Nineveh who could understand what animals said. The farmer once heard an ox lamenting to a donkey about how hard its life was. All day it had to labor, pulling the plow with no rest. It compared its life to the donkey's, which was pretty comfortable as it only had to carry their master occasionally and could relax most of the time. The donkey, wanting to help its friend, suggested that the ox pretend to be sick and unable to pull the plow the next day.

The ox heeded the donkey's advice and got a day of rest, but the donkey was forced to pull the plow on behalf of the ox. Exhausted, chafed, and sore, the donkey returned to the barn to find a satisfied ox, who declared the donkey to be its good friend for its wise advice. However, the donkey was bitter and angry about his unintended consequence and warned the ox never to act sick again or the master would send the ox to the butcher. Their friendship hence came to an end.

Mathon then explains the moral of story: If one chooses to help a friend out, help in a way which does not bring that friend's burden upon oneself.

After showing Rodan some of the collateral he's received from borrowers over the years and explaining their origin, Mathon teaches Rodan that there's never a 100% guarantee that people will repay their loans. What Rodan can do about his brother-in-law is to review his business proposal, and if deemed sensible, lend him his savings of one entire year, which is one piece of gold.

The financial counseling session concludes with Mathon imparting this piece of wisdom to Rodan: "Better a little caution than a great regret."

It's always hardest to say no to the people you're closest to. Actress Deidre Hall from Days Of Our Lives learnt that the hard way when she loaned her family (and some friends) approximately $800,000 when they ran into hard times, even taking out $150,000 from her pension plan. When her friend passed away, court action was needed in order for Hall to get her money back.

Radon's dilemma over lending his reward of fifty pieces of gold is relatable even in modern times now.

How often have your friends or family members approached you for "just a little bit to get by," or told you that they would "pay you back for sure"?

Half the time excuses are made or there's just not enough to pay you back, and you get a sense that you're being cheated of your trust (not to mention your money).

As Mathon advised, we should always consider the options and possibilities before we agree to lending anyone money, especially to friends and family. Shakespeare's Polonius said, "Neither a borrower nor a lender be; For loan oft loses both itself and friend," and there's a reason why these age-old tales in and out of this book still ring true today. When money comes between you and a loved one, it's hard to resolve the issue without some feelings being hurt or tempers flaring.

There are many reasons why we shouldn't lend money to our friends and family:

1. The loan has no deadline and hence not a priority for the borrower

When you lend money to a loved one, most times it's because they really need the money in a pinch, which makes it hard for you to set a date by when they should return it. And because there's no pressing deadline, no penalty charges or interest fees, repaying the loan gets put on the back burner.

2. It's hard to ask for the money back

Most likely the person you've lent money to is someone you cared about (or else you wouldn't have lent it in the first place), so it can be difficult to ask for the money back or even offer a gentle reminder, lest you make the borrower feel bad or like you're a calculative person.

3. The borrower may feel indebted to the lender

A lot of the time, the borrower feels indebted to the lender, and may say yes to favors or opinions whether they like it or not - their freedom of choice is seemingly taken away. It becomes a sort of master-servant relationship.

4. The lender becomes an enabler

Instead of tackling the root problem head-on, such as a gambling habit or lack of discipline in finances, your loan becomes an easy way out and continues the cycle of poor financial decisions.

5. The lender might need the money after all

Emergencies can hardly be predicted, and who knows when you might suddenly run into financial trouble? Loss of a job, unforeseen car or house repairs, sudden illness - all these can cause your financial stability to stumble.

The money you've loaned out can go a long way during your period of unemployment or medical leave.

Hence, there are a number of things to take note of before you lend anyone your hard-earned money:

🏛 **Step 1**: Find out the reasons for the loan. Is it for a new business venture? Or is it for something extravagant and unnecessary?

🏛 **Step 2**: If it's to start up a business, peruse the business proposal (or find someone who is savvy at this to take a look) to see if it's worth the risk. Ask the borrower how they plan on accomplishing their business goals. Ask for the specifics. Don't settle for vague answers like, "Oh, leave that to me," or "I know a guy."

🏛 **Step 3**: Draw up a promissory note - there are many free samples available online, such as www.lawdepot.com or even www.creditcards.com. These are legally binding and can offer you some security in getting your money back. (However, there's no 100% guarantee as well, depending on a number of factors when the note was made.) If your friend or family member refuses to sign a promissory note (provided the terms are reasonable, of course), it is a sign that you may have a hard time getting your money back from them in the future.

🏛 **Step 4**: Get some collateral if you can. Using something the borrower cherishes and uses regularly, such as an iPad or a laptop, can prove efficient in getting your loan money back as soon as possible. Relinquishing things like these shows how sincere the borrower is in paying you back, and provides an incentive for them to do so quickly.

🏛 **Step 5**: Ask yourself this: "Is it okay if I never see that money again?" If you don't think you can afford to lose that amount of money, it's best if you don't make the deal.

In the event the borrower doesn't return you the money, your relationship with them will become strained and even turn sour. Have an honest talk with the borrower to determine how you both will handle the relationship should negative circumstances arise. Sometimes talking things out beforehand will provide a clear perspective on whether the loan is worth risking the friendship or not.

If you've decided to loan the money, here are some tips to prevent any misunderstandings or unhappiness on both sides:

🏛 Propose a deadline and payment schedule. This proves that the borrower is intent on paying you back and will eliminate any grey areas about whether to ask for your money back, or let the loan go on indefinitely (while resentment and bitterness fester inside you).

🏛 Use gentle reminders instead of passive-aggressive remarks about how much the borrower has been spending lately. Sometimes it may just have slipped their minds! A gentle, perhaps humorous reminder will work better than a harsh rebuke any day.

🏛 Ask if they need any help in managing fiscal accounts or with budgeting. There are countless free budgeting tools available on the Internet or you can always go with the simpler all-cash methods.

🏛 If the borrower tends to skip out on payments due to budget constraints, you can try having them pay for you when you're out together. It's easier on their wallets to shell out a few bucks here and there for a meal, rather than a lump sum at the start of each month (or whatever payment schedule you've set up). This way you get to enjoy some "perks" as well!

THE WALLS OF BABYLON

Old Banzar, grim warrior of another day, stood guard at the passageway leading to the top of the ancient walls of Babylon. Up above, valiant defenders were battling to hold the walls. Upon them depended the future existence of this great city with its hundreds of thousands of citizens.

Over the walls came the roar of the attacking armies, the yelling of many men, the trampling of thousands of horses, the deafening boom of the battering rams pounding the bronzed gates.

In the street behind the gate lounged the spearmen, waiting to defend the entrance should the gates give way. They were but few for the task. The main armies of Babylon were with their king, far away in the east on the great expedition against the Elamites. No attack upon the city having been anticipated during their absence, the defending forces were small.

Unexpectedly, from the north, bore down the mighty armies of the Assyrians. And now the walls must hold or Babylon was doomed.

About Banzar were great crowds of citizens, white-faced and terrified, eagerly seeking news of the battle. With hushed awe they viewed the stream of wounded and dead being carried or led out of the passageway.

Here was the crucial point of attack. After three days of circling about the city, the enemy had suddenly thrown his great strength against this section and this gate.

The defenders from the top of the wall fought off the climbing platforms and the scaling ladders of the attackers with arrows, burning oil and, if any reached the top, spears. Against the defenders, thousands of the enemy's archers poured a deadly barrage of arrows.

Old Banzar had the vantage point for news. He was closest to the conflict and first to hear of each fresh repulse of the frenzied attackers.

An elderly merchant crowded close to him, his palsied hands quivering. "Tell me! Tell me!" he pleaded. "They cannot get in. My sons are with the good king. There is no one to protect my old wife.

My goods, they will steal all. My food, they will leave nothing. We are old, too old to defend ourselves—too old for slaves. We shall starve. We shall die. Tell me they cannot get in."

"Calm thyself, good merchant," the guard responded. "The walls of Babylon are strong. Go back to the bazaar and tell your wife that the walls will protect you and all of your possessions as safely as they protect the rich treasures of the king. Keep close to the walls, lest the arrows flying over strike you!"

A woman with a babe in arms took the old man's place as he withdrew. "Sergeant, what news from the top? Tell me truly that I may reassure my poor husband. He lies with fever from his terrible wounds, yet insists upon his armor and his spear to protect me, who am with child. Terrible he says will be the vengeful lust of our enemies should they break in."

"Be thou of good heart, thou mother that is, and is again to be, the walls of Babylon will protect you and your babes. They are high and strong. Hear ye not the yells of our valiant defenders as they empty the caldrons of burning oil upon the ladder scalers?"

"Yes, that do I hear and also the roar of the battering rams that do hammer at our gates."

"Back to thy husband. Tell him the gates are strong and withstand the rams. Also that the scalers climb the walls but to receive the waiting spear thrust. Watch, thy way and hasten behind you buildings."

Banzar stepped aside to clear the passage for heavily armed reinforcements. As, with clanking bronze shields and heavy tread, they tramped by, a small girl plucked at his girdle.

"Tell me please, soldier, are we safe?" she pleaded. I hear the awful noises. I see the men all bleeding. I am so frightened. What will become of our family, of my mother, little brother and the baby?"

The grim old campaigner blinked his eyes and thrust forward his chin as he beheld the child.

"Be not afraid, little one," he reassured her. "The walls of Babylon will protect you and mother and little brother and the baby. It was for the safety of such as you that the good Queen Semiramis built them over a hundred years ago. Never have they been broken through. Go back and tell your mother and little brother and the baby that the walls of Babylon will protect them and they need have no fear."

Day after day old Banzar stood at his post and watched the reinforcements file up the passageway, there to stay and fight until wounded or dead they came down once more. Around him, unceasingly crowded the throngs of frightened citizens eagerly seeking to learn if the walls would hold.

To all he gave his answer with the fine dignity of an old soldier, "The walls of Babylon will protect you."

For three weeks and five days the attack waged with scarcely ceasing violence. Harder and grimmer set the jaw of Banzar as the passage behind, wet with the blood of the many wounded, was churned into mud by the never ceasing streams of men passing up and staggering down. Each day the slaughtered attackers piled up in heaps before the wall. Each night they were carried back and buried by their comrades.

Upon the fifth night of the fourth week the clamor without diminished. The first streaks of daylight, illuminating the plains, disclosed great clouds of dust raised by the retreating armies.

A mighty shout went up from the defenders. There was no mistaking its meaning. It was repeated by the waiting troops behind the walls. It was echoed by the citizens upon the streets. It swept over the city with the violence of a storm.

People rushed from the houses. The streets were jammed with a throbbing mob. The pent-up fear of weeks found an outlet in the wild chorus of joy. From the top of the high tower of the Temple of Bel burst forth the flames of victory. Skyward floated the column of blue smoke to carry the message far and wide.

The walls of Babylon had once again repulsed a mighty and viscous foe determined to loot her rich treasures and to ravish and enslave her citizens. Babylon endured century after century because it was fully protected. It could not afford to be otherwise.

The walls of Babylon were an outstanding example of man's need and desire for protection. This desire is inherent in the human race. It is just as strong today as it ever was, but we have developed broader and better plans to accomplish the same purpose.

In this day, behind the impregnable walls of insurance, savings accounts and dependable investments, we can guard ourselves against the unexpected tragedies that may enter any door and seat themselves before any fireside.

We Cannot Afford To Be Without Adequate Protection

SUMMARY Guide

Babylon was under attack by the Assyrians, and war veteran Old Banzar was standing guard in a passageway that leads to the top of the walls. The defense force was greatly outnumbered as most of the Babylonian army were with the king on a distant expedition. If the walls fell, so would Babylon.

Many citizens were in a state of panic and clamored for Banzar's reassurance since he had a good view of the battle. Banzar calmly replies to each of them not to worry, and that the ancient walls of Babylon would stand firm.

After a few weeks of battle, the Assyrians retreated in defeat - Babylon's full and firm protection by its walls were the main cause of victory. These walls represent humans' innate need for protection today and one cannot afford to be left vulnerable to attacks in the form of, say, economical crises or natural disasters.

LEARNING / LESSON

This parable teaches us how it pays off to be well-prepared. Queen Semiramis built those walls well over a hundred years ago and they had never yielded to any attack over the years. She knew the treasures of Babylon would attract others to try and conquer the city, and she knew the power of having an impenetrable defense.

As we live today with our banks and investments, what can we do to build an impenetrable defense of our own treasures?

Like Babylon, we must protect our money wisely. And as Queen Semiramis did, we must secure our future by insuring our treasures now as well.

Before you make an investment, ask a trustworthy expert how to go about protecting your principal in it. There are many Principal-Protected investments on the market, but a lot of them incur high costs and by the time your stocks mature, your profits are practically insignificant.

Make sure to choose only those that offer protection with a high return rate. Many other types of stocks are also relatively low-risk and it's usually wise to diversify your portfolio, so don't be afraid to explore all options before you settle on something.

Insurance is a great and inexpensive way to obtain security for the future. A lot of people don't see the importance of insurance because they don't think long-term.

The wide range of insurance policies on the market now can offer you protection in a great many things: health, accidents, travel, theft, even loss of belongings.

You pay a small premium based on your potential risks and desired coverage, and you're protected against what you fear.

In the event something bad happens, at least your living expenses are covered for a while. And in life, something bad always happens eventually. One must be prepared for unforeseen circumstances. Have a safety net to fall back on.

Here are the types of insurance you should buy if you have the means to make the premium payments:

🏛 **Health insurance** (when you're in your 20s)

Healthcare without insurance is extremely expensive nowadays, even with the Affordable Care Act. This type of insurance is a perpetual need because as you grow older, the higher the chance you'll need more medical care. A whopping 44.3 million people in the US have no health insurance at all. Thus many people delay seeking medical attention due to fear of medical bills, leading to higher costs when the conditions worsen. If you can afford it, get it.

🏛 **Auto insurance** (if you get a car)

According to the National Highway Traffic Safety Administration (NHTSA), more than 5.6 million motor vehicle accidents were reported in 2013. Auto insurance rates can vary depending on driving history and a few other factors, but nothing compares to the nightmare of not having auto insurance when you need it. Even if you're a safe driver, you can't guarantee that everyone on the road is!

🏛 **Disability insurance** (when you have a job)

This type of insurance aims to provide for your living expenses if you become disabled and unable to work. If you are living on your income, you need this. If you have any dependants, you'll need this even more.

🏛 **Renter's insurance** (when you're renting a place)

For an extra $30 or so per month, you can get coverage for fires, leaks, or storms and other applicable unforeseen disasters. Remunerations for your damaged personal belongings are also included, along with costs for a temporary living situation in case your rented place is unfit to stay.

🏛 **Life insurance** (when you get married or have children)

Life insurance is meant to replace your income in the event of death, especially if you have dependants. You can set the policy to mature when your children are most likely to become financially independent. Lifehappens.org has a calculator to determine how much coverage you should be getting.

🏛 **Homeowner's insurance** (when you buy your own home)

This is a must for every homeowner as it covers everything from the building structure to injuries inflicted while in your home.

*T*HE CAMEL TRADER OF BABYLON

The hungrier one becomes, the clearer one's mind works— also the more sensitive one becomes to the odors of food.

Tarkad, the son of Azure, certainly thought so. For two whole days he had tasted no food except two small figs purloined from over the wall of a garden. Not another could he grab before the angry woman rushed forth and chased him down the street. Her shrill cries were still ringing in his ears as he walked through the market place. They helped him to retrain his restless fingers from snatching the tempting fruits from the baskets of the market women.

Never before had he realized how much food was brought to the markets of Babylon and how good it smelled. Leaving the market, he walked across to the inn and paced back and forth in front of the eating house.

Perhaps here he might meet someone he knew; someone from whom he could borrow a copper that would gain him a smile from the unfriendly keeper of the inn and, with it, a liberal helping. Without the copper he knew all too well how unwelcome he would be.

In his abstraction he unexpectedly found himself face to face with the one man he wished most to avoid, the tall bony figure of Dabasir, the camel trader. Of all the friends and others from whom he had borrowed small sums, Dabasir made him feel the most uncomfortable because of his failure to keep his promises to repay promptly.

Dabasir's face lighted up at the sight of him. "Ha! 'Tis Tarkad, just the one I have been seeking that he might repay the two pieces of copper which I lent him a moon ago; also the piece of silver which I lent to him before that. We are well met. I can make good use of the coins this very day. What say, boy? What say?"

Tarkad stuttered and his face flushed. He had naught in his empty stomach to nerve him to argue with the outspoken Dabasir. "I am sorry, very sorry," he mumbled weakly, "but this day I have neither the copper nor the silver with which I could repay." "Then get it," Dabasir insisted. "Surely thou canst get hold of a few coppers and a piece of silver to repay the generosity of an old friend of thy father who aided thee whenst thou wast in need?"

"Tis because ill fortune does pursue me that I cannot pay."

"Ill fortune! Wouldst blame the gods for thine own weakness. Ill fortune pursues every man who thinks more of borrowing than of repaying. Come with me, boy, while I eat. I am hungry and I would tell thee a tale."

Tarkad flinched from the brutal frankness of Dabasir, but here at least was an invitation to enter the coveted doorway of the eating house.

Dabasir pushed him to a far corner of the room where they seated themselves upon small rugs.

When Kauskor, the proprietor, appeared smiling, Dabasir addressed him with his usual freedom, "Fat lizard of the desert, bring to me a leg of the goat, brown with much juice, and bread and all of the vegetables for I am hungry and want much food. Do not forget my friend here. Bring to him a jug of water. Have it cooled, for the day is hot."

Tarkad's heart sank. Must he sit here and drink water while he watched this man devour an entire goat leg? He said nothing. He thought of nothing he could say.

Dabasir, however, knew no such thing as silence. Smiling and waving his hand good-naturedly to the other customers, all of whom knew him, he continued. "I did hear from a traveler just returned from Urfa of a certain rich man who has a piece of stone cut so thin that one can look through it. He put it in the window of his house to keep out the rains.

It is yellow, so this traveler does relate, and he was permitted to look through it and all the outside world looked strange and not like it really is. What say you to that, Tarkad? Thinkest all the world could look to a man a different color from what it is?"

"I dare say," responded the youth, much more interested in the fat leg of goat placed before Dabasir.

"Well, I know it to be true for I myself have seen the world all of a different color from what it really is and the tale I am about to tell relates how I came to see it in its right color once more."

Dabasir will tell a tale," whispered a neighboring diner to his neighbor, and dragged his rug close. Other diners brought their food and crowded in a semi-circle. They crunched noisily in the ears of Tarkad and brushed him with their meaty bones. He alone was without food. Dabasir did not offer to share with him nor even motion him to a small corner of the hard bread that was broken off and had fallen from the platter to the floor.

"The tale that I am about to tell," began Dabasir, pausing to bite a goodly chunk from the goat leg, "relates to my early life and how I came to be a camel trader. Didst anyone know that I once was a slave in Syria?"

A murmur of surprise ran through the audience to which Dabasir listened with satisfaction.

"When I was a young man," continued Dabasir after another vicious onslaught on the goat leg,

"I learned the trade of my father, the making of saddles. I worked with him in his shop and took to myself a wife.

Being young and not greatly skilled, I could earn but little, just enough to support my excellent wife in a modest way. I craved good things which I could not afford.

Soon I found that the shop keepers would trust me to pay later even though I could not pay at the time. "Being young and without experience I did not know that he who spends more than he earns is sowing the winds of needless self-indulgence from which he is sure to reap the whirlwinds of trouble and humiliation. So I indulged my whims for fine raiment and bought luxuries for my good wife and our home, beyond our means. "I paid as I could and for a while all went well. But in time I discovered I could not use my earnings both to live upon and to pay my debts.

Creditors began to pursue me to pay for my extravagant purchases and my life became miserable. I borrowed from my friends, but could not repay them either. Things went from bad to worse. My wife returned to her father and I decided to leave Babylon and seek another city where a young man might have better chances.

"For two years I had a restless and unsuccessful life working for caravan traders. From this I fell in with a set of likeable robbers who scoured the desert for unarmed caravans. Such deeds were unworthy of the son of my
father, but I was seeing the world through a colored stone and did not realize to what degradation I had fallen.

"We met with success on our first trip, capturing a rich haul of gold and silks and valuable merchandise. This loot we took to Ginir and squandered.

"The second time we were not so fortunate. Just after we had made our capture, we were attacked by the spearsmen of a native chief to whom the caravans paid for protection. Our two leaders were killed, and the rest of us were taken to Damascus where we were stripped of our clothing and sold as slaves.

"I was purchased for two pieces of silver by a Syrian desert chief. With my hair shorn and but a loin cloth to wear, I was not so different from the other slaves.

Being a reckless youth, I thought it merely an adventure until my master took me before his four wives and told them they could have me for a eunuch.

Then, indeed, did I realize the hopelessness of my situation. These men of the desert were fierce and warlike. I was subject to their will without weapons or means of escape.

"Fearful I stood, as those four women looked me over. I wondered if I could expect pity from them. Sira, the first wife, was older than the others. Her face was impassive as she looked upon me. I turned from her with little consolation. The next was a contemptuous beauty who gazed at me as indifferently as if I had been a worm of the earth. The two younger ones tittered as though it were all an exciting joke.

"It seemed an age that I stood waiting sentence. Each woman appeared willing for the others to decide. Finally Sira spoke up in a cold voice.

"Of eunuchs we have plenty, but of camel tenders we have few and they are a worthless lot.

Even this day I would visit my mother who is sick with the fever and there is no slave I would trust to lead my camel. Ask this slave if he can lead a camel.'

"My master thereupon questioned me, 'What know you of camels?'

"Striving to conceal my eagerness, I replied, I can make them kneel, I can load them, I can lead them on long trips without tiring. If need be, I can repair their trappings."

"The slave speaks forward enough, observed my master. If thou so desire, Sira, take this man for thy camel tender.'

"So I was turned over to Sira and that day I led her camel upon a long journey to her sick mother.

I took the occasion to thank her for her intercession and also to tell her that I was not a slave by birth, but the son of a freeman, an honorable saddle maker of Babylon. I also told her much of my story. Her comments were disconcerting to me and I pondered much afterwards on what she said.

"How can you call yourself a free man when your weakness has brought you to this? If a man has in himself the soul of a slave will he not become one no matter what his birth, even as water seeks its level? If a man has within him the soul of a free man, will he not become respected and honored in his own city in spite of his misfortune?'

"For over a year I was a slave and lived with the slaves, but I could not become as one of them.

One day Sira asked me, 'In the eventime when the other slaves can mingle and enjoy the society of each other, why dost thou sit in thy tent alone?'

"To which I responded, 'I am pondering what you have said to me. I wonder if I have the soul of a slave. I cannot join them, so I must sit apart.'

"I, too, must sit apart,' she confided. 'My dowry was large and my lord married me because of it. Yet he does not desire me. What every woman longs for is to be desired. Because of this and because I am barren and have neither son nor daughter, must I sit apart. Were I a man I would rather die than be such a slave, but the conventions of our tribe make slaves of women.'

"What think thou of me by this time?' I asked her suddenly, 'Have I the soul of a man or have I the soul of a slave?'

"Have you a desire to repay the just debts you owe in Babylon?' she parried.

"Yes, I have the desire, but I see no way.'

"If thou contentedly let the years slip by and make no effort to repay, then thou hast but the contemptible soul of a slave. No man is otherwise who cannot respect himself and no man can respect himself who does not repay honest debts.'

"But what can I do who am a slave in Syria?'

"Stay a slave in Syria, thou weakling.'

"I am not a weakling,' I denied hotly.

"Then prove it.'

"How?'

"Does not thy great king fight his enemies in every way he can and with every force he has?

Thy debts are thy enemies. They ran thee out of Babylon. You left them alone and they grew too strong for thee. Hadst fought them as a man, thou couldst have conquered them and been one honored among the townspeople. But thou had not the soul to fight them and behold thy pride hast gone down until thou art a slave in Syria.'

"Much I thought over her unkind accusations and many defensive phrases I worded to prove myself not a slave at heart, but I was not to have the chance to use them. Three days later the maid of Sira took me to her mistress.

"My mother is again very sick,' she said. 'Saddle the two best camels in my husband's herd. Tie on water skins and saddle bags for a long journey. The maid will give thee food at the kitchen tent.' I packed the camels wondering much at the quantity of provisions the maid provided, for the mother dwelt less than a day's journey away.

The maid rode the rear camel which followed and I led the camel of my mistress. When we reached her mother's house it was just dark. Sira dismissed the maid and said to me:

"Dabasir, hast thou the soul of a free man or the soul of a slave?' "The soul of a free man,' I insisted.

"Now is thy chance to prove it. Thy master hath imbibed deeply and his chiefs are in a stupor.

Take then these camels and make thy escape. Here in this bag is raiment of
thy master's to disguise thee. I will say thou stole the camels and ran away while I visited my sick mother.'

"Thou hast the soul of a queen,' I told her. 'Much do I wish that I might lead thee to happiness.'

"Happiness,' she responded, 'awaits not the runaway wife who seeks it in far lands among strange people. Go thy own way and may the gods of the desert protect thee for the way is far and barren of food or water.'

"I needed no further urging, but thanked her warmly and was away into the night. I knew not this strange country and had only a dim idea of the direction in which lay Babylon, but struck out bravely across the desert toward the hills. One camel I rode and the other I led. All that night I traveled and all the next day, urged on by the knowledge of the terrible fate that was meted out to slaves who stole their master's property and tried to escape.

"Late that afternoon, I reached a rough country as uninhabitable as the desert. The sharp rocks bruised the feet of my faithful camels and soon they were picking their way slowly and painfully along.

I met neither man nor beast and could well understand why they shunned this inhospitable land.

"It was such a journey from then on as few men live to tell of. Day after day we plodded along.

Food and water gave out. The heat of the sun was merciless. At the end of the ninth day, I slid from the back of my mount with the feeling that I was too weak to ever remount and I would surely die, lost in this abandoned country.

"I stretched out upon the ground and slept, not waking until the first gleam of daylight.

"I sat up and looked about me. There was a coolness in the morning air. My camels lay dejected not far away. About me was a vast waste of broken country covered with rock and sand and thorny things, no sign of water, naught to eat for man or camel.

"Could it be that in this peaceful quiet I faced my end? My mind was clearer than it had ever been before. My body now seemed of little importance. My parched and bleeding lips, my dry and swollen tongue, my empty stomach, all had lost their supreme agonies of the day before.

"I looked across into the uninviting distance and once again came to me the question, 'Have I the soul of a slave or the soul of a free man?' Then with clearness I realized that if I had the soul of a slave, I should give up, lie down in the desert and die, a fitting end for a runaway slave.

"But if I had the soul of a free man, what then? Surely I would force my way back to Babylon, repay the people who had trusted me, bring happiness to my wife who truly loved me and bring peace and contentment to my parents.

"Thy debts are thine enemies who have run thee out of Babylon,' Sira had said. Yes it was so.

Why had I refused to stand my ground like a man? Why had I permitted my wife to go back to her father?

"Then a strange thing happened. All the world seemed to be of a different color as though I had been looking at it through a colored stone which had suddenly been removed. At last I saw the true values in life.

"Die in the desert! Not I! With a new vision, I saw the things that I must do.

First I would go back to Babylon and face every man to whom I owed an unpaid debt. I should tell them that after years of wandering and misfortune, I had come back to pay my debts as fast as the gods would permit. Next I should make a home for my wife and become a citizen of whom my parents should be proud.

"My debts were my enemies, but the men I owed were my friends for they had trusted me and believed in me.

"I staggered weakly to my feet. What mattered hunger? What mattered thirst? They were but incidents on the road to Babylon. Within me surged the soul of a free man going back to conquer his enemies and reward his friends. I thrilled with the great resolve.

"The glazed eyes of my camels brightened at the new note in my husky voice. With great effort, after many attempts, they gained their feet. With pitiful perseverance, they pushed on toward the north where something within me said we would find Babylon.

"We found water. We passed into a more fertile country where were grass and fruit. We found the trail to Babylon because the soul of a free man looks at life as a series of problems to be solved and solves them, while the soul of a slave whines, 'What can I do who am but a slave?'

"How about thee, Tarkad? Dost thy empty stomach make thy head exceedingly clear? Art ready to take the road that leads back to self respect? Canst thou see the world in its true color? Hast thou the desire to pay thy honest debts, however many they may be, and once again be a man respected in Babylon?"

Moisture came to the eyes of the youth. He rose eagerly to his knees. "Thou has shown me a vision; already I feel the soul of a free man surge within me."

"But how fared you upon your return?" questioned an interested listener.

"Where the determination is, the way can be found" Dabasir replied. "I now had the determination so I set out to find a way.

First I visited every man to whom I was indebted and begged his indulgence until I could earn that with which to repay. Most of them met me gladly. Several reviled me but others offered to help me; one indeed did give me the very help I needed. It was Mathon, the gold lender.

Learning that I had been a camel tender in Syria; he sent me to old Nebatur, the camel trader, just commissioned by our good king to purchase many herds of sound camels for the great expedition. With him, my knowledge of camels I put to good use. Gradually I was able to repay every copper and every piece of silver. Then at last I could hold up my head and feel that I was an honourable man among men."

Again Dabasir turned to his food. "Kauskor, thou snail," he called loudly to be heard in the kitchen, "the food is cold. Bring me more meat fresh from the roasting. Bring thou also a very large portion for Tarkad, the son of my old friend, who is hungry and shall eat with me."

So ended the tale of Dabasir the camel trader of old Babylon. He found his own soul when he realized a great truth, a truth that had been known and used by wise men long before his time. It has led men of all ages out of difficulties and into success and it will continue to do so for those who have the wisdom to understand its magic power. It is for any man to use who reads these lines.

Where The Determination Is, The Way Can Be Found

SUMMARY
Guide

Tarkad, starving and roaming the streets, unexpectedly came across Dabasir the camel trader at the market who then asked about the coins which he owed for some time.

Unable to return, Tarkad apologized to Dabasir who then invited him to the eating house. As the camel trader ordered food, he offered an anecdote of how a traveler put up a piece of stone in his house window to keep out the rain. Because of the yellow color of the stone, the exterior view suddenly looked different. Although Dabasir asked Tarkad his opinion, the latter was more interested in the food which the camel trader ordered.

Dabasir began his story:

When Dabasir was young, he learned the trade of saddle making from his father. Subsequently he started earning money, and then indulged excessively. He even put himself on credit through moneylenders - until his debts snowballed. The situation turned so bad that his wife returned to her father while Dabasir decided to leave Babylon to seek better fortunes.

Dabasir joined caravan traders and started a life of theft. However he was soon captured by the spearsmen who were protecting some caravans they robbed. He was thereafter purchased by a Syrian desert chief and presented to his wives as a potential eunuch.

However none of the wives were interested in Dabasir. The first wife Sira decided to keep him as a camel trader when he convinced her of his superior knowledge. Dabasir revealed the truth that he was a free man and not a slave, although Sira sneered at him for succumbing to his fate so easily, leaving Dabasir to ponder over their conversation.

The opportunity came when Sira required a journey to visit her sick mother. Dabasir was picked to accompany Sira. When they reached her mother's place, Sira told Dabasir to take the camels and escape.

However, the desert was a tough place, and Dabasir eventually succumbed to the arduous journey, having also exhausted his food and water. At a critical moment, he roused himself from near death because of his will to live, and eventually came across fertile land and water and grass, and the route to Babylon.

Once back at Babylon, Dabasir met up with the moneylenders whom he owed money and came to a agreement with most of them. Through Mathon the moneylender, Dabasir was sent to Nebatur to work, and eventually starting his own business and earning more than enough to clear his debts.

LEARNING/LESSON

Because Dabasir did not keep track of his own frivolous expenditures, he quickly ran into debt, especially when he couldn't afford his lifestyle on credit.

Even today, we still see lots of people facing daunting issues in clearing their credit card debts.

For instance, in a June 2015 report by Cardhub, it was revealed that consumers paid more than $57 billion in new debts in the year 2014, with an average household balance of $7,177.

According to their projection for the year 2015, the total credit card debt would amount up to about $55.8 billion. We don't have to look far for an example of a person plagued with a huge debt.

Lindsay Lohan, famous wild-child, who recently completed her 125 hours of court-ordered community service, reportedly owed $600,000 in credit card debts back in 2010.

Although she is a movie star, her wild partying ways and the dismal acting career back then meant that her income was substantially lacking.

In addition, she was supposedly 2 months behind her rent at one point in time, with the landlord serving her a legal notice for her late rent. The ultimatum was to pay or move out. Due to that, Lindsay Lohan had to reportedly pay $23,000 to prevent being reduced to a homeless fate.

At the time of writing, it is still unclear whether she cleared her debts.

With credit cards being easy to qualify for and obtain, many people are now simply signing their purchases at a daily whim. While many do keep track of their expenses, equally many throw caution to the wind, believing that they have no problem.

But there are some simple measures you can implement to make sure your credit card debts don't snowball and cause an avalanche !

🏛 **Establish A Budget** - It looks rather easy. Establish a budget. Follow that budget, exactly. If you don't have the budget for it for this month, then don't charge it!

🏛 **The Credit Balance Is Not To Exceed Longer Than 6 Months -** Beyond this duration, experts point out that the compounding of simple interest can create an expensive balance to pay off.

🏛 **The Rewards' Credit Cards -** Cardholders usually end up spending more than the rewards itself, if they don't pay attention to the associated card fees or interest.

🏛 **Low-Interest Credit Card -** Get a low-interest one especially if you find your credit card's interest card too excessive.

🏛 **Avoid Balance Transfers -** Don't transfer for the sake of transferring. If you do transfer, it is only for a good reason, for instance, to take advantage of a low interest rate. otherwise, your balance will simply increase, also because of the balance transfer fee.

BONUS TIP - Limit The Number Of Cards!

Usually people just sign up for credit cards due to some attractive promotion the banks might be having that particular day. And believe it or not, some just want the promotional gift or vouchers etc that are given out. The more cards you have, the more you can, and WILL, charge.

You may feel you have self-control, but it is better not to tempt yourself with the thousands of dollars in available credit (when you add up the credit from the all the cards).

If you do feel you need all those cards, limit the number you keep in your wallet. Take a look at the cards you have now - Are there any that you hardly use at all? Cancel it. You don't really need it!

THE CLAY TABLETS FROM BABYLON.

St. Swithin's College

Nottingham University

Newark-on-Trent

Nottingham

Professor Franklin Caldwell,

Care of British Scientific Expedition,

Hillah, Mesopotamia.

October 21, 1934.

My dear Professor:

The five clay tablets from your recent excavation in the ruins of Babylon arrived on the same boat with your letter. I have been fascinated no end, and have spent many pleasant hours translating their inscriptions. I should have answered your letter at once but delayed until I could complete the translations which are attached.

The tablets arrived without damage, thanks to your careful use of preservatives and excellent packing.

You will be as astonished as we in the laboratory at the story they relate. One expects the dim and distant past to speak of romance and adventure. "Arabian Nights" sort of things, you know.

When instead it discloses the problem of a person named Dabasir to pay off his debts, one realizes that conditions upon this old world have not changed as much in five thousand years as one might expect.

It's odd, you know , but these old inscriptions rather "rage" me, as the students say. Being a college professor, I am supposed to be a thinking human being possessing a working knowledge of most subjects.

Yet, here comes this old chap out of the dust-covered ruins of Babylon to offer a way I had never heard of to pay off my debts and at the same time acquire gold to jingle in my wallet.

Pleasant thought, I say, and interesting to prove whether it will work as well nowadays as it did in old Babylon. Mrs. Shrewsbury and myself are planning to try out his plan upon our own affairs which could be much improved. Wishing you the best of luck in your worthy undertaking and waiting eagerly another opportunity to assist, I am

Yours sincerely,

Alfred H. Shewsbury,

Department of Archaeology.

TABLET NO. I

Now, when the moon becometh full, I, Dabasir, who am but recently returned from slavery in Syria, with the determination to pay my many just debts and become a man of means worthy of respect in my native city of Babylon, do here engrave upon the clay a permanent record of my affairs to guide and assist me in carrying through my high desires.

Under the wise advice of my good friend Mathon, the gold lender, I am determined to follow an exact plan that he doth say will lead any honorable man out of debt into means and self respect.

This plan includeth three purposes which are my hope and desire.

First, the plan doth provide for my future prosperity.

Therefore one-tenth of all I earn shall be set aside as my own to keep. For Mathon speaketh wisely when he saith:

"That man who keepeth in his purse both gold and silver that he need not spend is good to his family and loyal to his king.

"The man who hath but a few coppers in his purse is indifferent to his family and indifferent to his king.

"But the man who hath naught in his purse is unkind to his family and is disloyal to his king, for his own heart is bitter.

"Therefore, the man who wisheth to achieve must have coin that he may keep to jingle in his purse, that he have in his heart love for his family and loyalty to his king."

Second, the plan doth provide that I shall support and clothe my good wife who hath returned to me with loyalty from the house of her father. For Mathon doth say that to take good care of a faithful wife putteth self-respect into the heart of a man and addeth strength and determination to his purposes.

Therefore seven-tenths of all I earn shall be used to provide a home, clothes to wear, and food to eat, with a bit extra to spend, that our lives be not lacking in pleasure and enjoyment. But he doth further enjoin the greatest care that we spend not greater than seven-tenths of what I earn for these worthy purposes. Herein lieth the success of the plan.

I must live upon this portion and never use more nor buy what I may not pay for out of this portion.

TABLET NO. II

Third, the plan doth provide that out of my earnings my debts shall be paid. Therefore each time the moon is full, two-tenths of all I have earned shall be divided honourably and fairly among those who have trusted me and to whom I am indebted. Thus in due time will all my indebtedness be surely paid.

Therefore, do I here engrave the name of every man to whom I am indebted and the honest amount of my debt.

Fahru, the cloth weaver, 2 silver, 6 copper. Sinjar, the couch maker, 1 silver.

Ahmar, my friend, 3 silver, 1 copper. Zankar, my friend, 4 silver, 7 copper, Askamir, my friend, 1 silver, 3 copper.

Harinsir, the Jewelmaker, 6 silver, 2 copper. Diarbeker, my father's friend, 4 silver, 1 copper. Alkahad, the house owner, 14 silver.

Mathon, the gold lender, 9 silver. Birejik, the farmer, 1 silver, 7 copper. (From here on, disintegrated. Cannot be deciphered.)

TABLET NO. III

To these creditors do I owe in total one hundred and nineteen pieces of silver and one hundred and forty-one pieces of copper. Because I did owe these sums and saw no way to repay, in my folly I did permit my wife to return to her father and didst leave my native city and seek easy wealth elsewhere, only to find disaster and to see myself sold into the degradation of slavery.

Now that Mathon doth show me how I can repay my debts in small sums of my earnings, do I realize the great extent of my folly in running away from the results of my extravagances. Therefore have I visited my creditors and explained to them that I have no resources with which to pay except my ability to earn, and that I intent to apply two tenths of all I earn upon my indebtedness evenly and honestly. This much can I pay but no more.

Therefore if they be patient, in time my obligations will be paid in full.

Ahmar, whom I thought my best friend, reviled me bitterly and I left him in humiliation.

Birejik, the farmer, pleaded that I pay him first as he didst badly need help.

Alkahad, the house owner, was indeed disagreeable and insisted that he would make me trouble unless I didst soon settle in full with him.

All the rest willingly accepted my proposal. Therefore am I more determined than ever to carry through, being convinced that it is easier to pay one's just debts than to avoid them. Even though I cannot meet the needs and demands of a few of my creditors I will deal impartially with all.

TABLET NO. IV

Again the moon shines full. I have worked hard with a free mind. My good wife hath supported my intentions to pay my creditors. Because of our wise determination, I have earned during the past moon, buying camels of sound wind and good legs, for Nebatur, the sum of nineteen pieces of silver.

This I have divided according to the plan. One-tenth have I set aside to keep as my own, seven-tenths have I divided with my good wife to pay for our living. Two-tenths have I divided among my creditors as evenly as could be done in coppers.

I did not see Ahmar but left it with his wife. Birejik was so pleased he would kiss my hand. Old Alkahad alone was grouchy and said I must pay faster. To which I replied that if I were permitted to be well fed and not worried, that alone would enable me to pay faster. All the others thanked me and spoke well of my efforts.

Therefore, at the end of one moon, my indebtedness is reduced by almost four pieces of silver and I possess almost two pieces of silver besides, upon which no man hath claim. My heart is lighter than it hath been for a long time.

Again the moon shines full. I have worked hard but with poor success. Few camels have I been able to buy. Only eleven pieces of silver have I earned. Nevertheless my good wife and I have stood by the plan even though we have bought no new raiment and eaten little but herbs.

Again I paid ourselves one-tenth of the eleven pieces, while we lived upon seven-tenths. I was surprised when Ahmar commended my payment, even though small. So did Birejik. Alkahad flew into a rage but when told to give back his portion if he did not wish it, he became reconciled.

The others, as before, were content Again the moon shines full and I am greatly rejoiced. I intercepted a fine herd of camels and bought many sound ones, therefore my earnings were forty-two pieces of silver. This moon my wife and myself have bought much needed sandals and raiment Also we have dined well on meat and fowl.

More than eight pieces of silver we have paid to our creditors. Even Alkahad did not protest.

Great is the plan for it leadeth us out of debt and giveth us wealth which is ours to keep.

Three times the moon had been full since I last carved upon this clay. Each time I paid to myself one-tenth of all I earned. Each time my good wife and I have lived upon seven-tenths even though at times it was difficult. Each time have I paid to my creditors two-tenths.

In my purse I now have twenty one pieces of silver that are mine. It maketh my head to stand straight upon my shoulders and maketh me proud to walk
among my friends. My wife keepeth well our home and is becomingly gowned. We are happy to live together.

The plan is of untold value. Hath it not made an honorable man of an ex-slave?

TABLET NO. V

Again the moon shines full and I remember that it is long since I carved upon the clay. Twelve moons in truth have come and gone. But this day I will not neglect my record because upon this day I have paid the last of my debts.

This is the day upon which my good wife and my thankful self celebrate with great feasting that our determination hath been achieved.

Many things occurred upon my final visit to my creditors that I shall long remember. Ahmar begged my forgiveness for his unkind words and said that I was one of all others he most desired for a friend.

Old Alkahad is not so bad after all, for he said, "Thou wert once a piece of soft clay to be pressed and moulded by any hand that touched thee, but now thou art a piece of bronze capable of holding an edge. If thou needst silver or gold at any time come to me."

Nor is he the only one who holdeth me in high regard. Many others speak deferentially to me.

My good wife looketh upon me with a light in her eyes that doth make a man have confidence in himself.

Yet it is the plan that hath made my success. It hath enabled me to pay all my debts and to jingle both gold and silver in my purse. I do commend it to all who wish to get ahead. For truly if it will enable an ex-slave to pay his debts and have gold in his purse, will it not aid any man to find independence? Nor am I, myself, finished with it, for I am convinced that if I follow it further it will make me rich among men.

St. Swithin's College

Nottingham University

Newark-on-Trent

Nottingham
Professor Franklin Caldwell,

Care of British Scientific Expedition,

Hillah, Mesopotamia.

November 7th, 1936.

My dear professor:

If, in your further digging into those ruins of Babylon, you encounter the ghost of a former resident, an old camel trader named Dabasir, do me a favor.

Tell him that his scribbling upon those clay tablets, so long ago, has earned for him the lifelong gratitude of a couple of college folks back here in England.

You will possibly remember my writing a year ago that Mrs. Shrewsbury and myself intended to try his plan for getting out of debt and at the same time having gold to jingle. You may have guessed, even though we tried to keep it from our friends, our desperate straits.

We were frightfully humiliated for years by a lot of old debts and worried sick for fear some of the trades-people might start a scandal that would force me out of the college. We paid and paid—every shilling we could squeeze out of income—but it was hardly enough to hold things even. Besides we were forced to do all our buying where we could get further credit regardless of higher costs.

It developed into one of those vicious circles that grow worse instead of better. Our struggles were getting hopeless. We could not move to less costly rooms because we owed the landlord. There did not appear to be anything we could do to improve our situation.

Then, here comes your acquaintance, the old camel trader from Babylon, with a plan to do just what we wished to accomplish. He jolly well stirred us up to follow his system. We made a list of all our debts and I took it around and showed it to everyone we owed.

I explained how it was simply impossible for me to ever pay them the way things were going along. They could readily see this themselves from the figures. Then I explained that the only way I saw to pay in full was to set aside twenty percent of my income each month to be divided pro rata, which would pay them in full in a little over two years. That, in the meantime, we would go on a cash basis and give them the further benefit of our cash purchases.

They were really quite decent. Our greengrocer, a wise old chap, put it in a way that helped to bring around the rest. "If you pay for all you buy and then pay some on what you owe, that is better than you have done, for ye ain't paid down the account none in three years." Finally I secured all their names to an agreement binding them not to molest us as long as the twenty percent of income was paid regularly.

Then we began scheming on how to live upon seventy percent. We were determined to keep that extra ten percent to jingle. The thought of silver and possibly gold was most alluring.

It was like having an adventure to make the change. We enjoyed figuring this way and that, to live comfortably upon that remaining seventy percent. We started with rent and managed to secure a fair reduction.

Next we put our favorite brands of tea and such under suspicion and were agreeably surprised how often we could purchase superior qualities at less cost.

It is too long a story for a letter but anyhow it did not prove difficult. We managed and right cheerfully at that. What a relief it proved to have our affairs in such a shape we were no longer persecuted by past due accounts.

I must not neglect, however, to tell you about that extra ten percent we were supposed to jingle. Well, we did jingle it for some time. Now don't laugh too soon. You see, that is the sporty part. It is the real fun, to start accumulating money that you do not want to spend.

There is more pleasure in running up such a surplus than there could be in spending it.

After we had jingled to our hearts' content, we found a more profitable use for it. We took up an investment upon which we could pay that ten percent each month. This is proving to be the most satisfying part of our regeneration. It is the first thing we pay out of my check.

There is a most gratifying sense of security to know our investment is growing steadily. By the time my teaching days are over it should be a snug sum, large enough so the income will take care of us from then on.

All this out of my same old check. Difficult to believe, yet absolutely true. All our debts being gradually paid and at the same time our investment increasing. Besides we get along, financially, even better than before. Who would believe there could be such a difference in results between following a financial plan and just drifting along.

At the end of the next year, when all our old bills shall have been paid, we will have more to pay upon our investment besides some extra for travel.

We are determined never again to permit our living expenses to exceed seventy percent of our income. Now you can understand why we would like to extend our personal thanks to that old chap whose plan saved us from our "Hell on Earth."

He knew. He had been through it all. He wanted others to benefit from his own bitter experiences. That is why he spent tedious hours

carving his message upon the clay. He had a real message for fellow sufferers, a message so important that after five thousand years it has risen out of the ruins of Babylon, just as true and just as vital as the day it was buried.

Yours sincerely,

Alfred H. Shrewsbury,

Department of Archaeology.

SUMMARY
Guide

Alfred Shrewsbury, from the Department of Archaeology, received a set of tablets from Professor Franklin Caldwell of St. Swithin's College, Nottingham University.

Upon translating the inscriptions on the Babylonian-age tablet, Alfred Shrewsbury was doubly fascinated - because it revealed the story of an individual named Dabasir who was greatly in debt - a situation which he was also experiencing!

This Dabasir was also the same man who appeared in the previous story "The Camel Trader of Babylon".

According to the inscriptions, Dabasir basically followed 3 concepts:

Assign 1/10 aside for savings.

Assign 7/10 for household expenditure.

Assign 2/10 to clear all existing debts.

And eventually, Dabasir did clear his debts.

Inspired, Alfred decided to follow the inscribed instructions as much as he could, to clear his debts, and he succeeded too.

This chapter features 3 concepts as listed out in the Summary:

🏛 Savings.

🏛 Household Expenditure Budget.

🏛 Debt Clearance.

We will go through each of them here.

#1: Savings

Previously, we shared strategies on savings, like the plain old savings accounts and T. Harv Eker's money jar concept. Now, we'll look at something different which can also help - apps.

Yes, apps!

In this time of the day, many of us often use apps on a daily basis. Therefore, it would be more practical to make use of that oft-used gadget - the cellphone.

Here are 2 apps for your consideration:

Name: Mint

Where: www.mint.com

Cost: FREE

Available For: iOS and Android

Description: This power-packed app is designed to help you plan your spending in a smarter way, thereby enhancing your savings.

By keeping track of ALL your financial activity from ALL your accounts, cards and investments, you are able to create budgets and organize your various accounts to better enhance tracking of expenses.

Name: You Need A Budget (YNAB)

Where: www.youneedabudget.com/features/iphone

Cost: FREE

Available For: iOS and Android

Description: This app works on a few simple rules of engagement. First, it gives every dollar a job. Second, it provides the platform to save for a rainy day.

BONUS TIP: Groupon

If you haven't heard of Groupon (www.groupon.com), where have you been hiding under all this while?

The website is a global e-commerce market place, offering millions of deals to subscribers, such as travel, classes, services, souvenirs and more other great and diverse deals!

Importantly, the offers easily range from 50% to 90%, so it can help you manage your money better!

#2: Household Expenditure Budget

With your earnings separated into their various uses, you now have less you can spend on the household. Would the quality of life be reduced as a result of that?

Nope, not at all. Especially if you can plan and budget smartly.

Here are 2 apps for your consideration:

Name: Grocery iQ

Where: www.groceryiq.com

Cost: FREE

Available For: iOS and Android

Description: The app is one intuitive and easy shopping list you would be pleased to use. There are features with barcode scanning and predictive search in the app's database. With this platform, you would be able to stay on task while shopping and avoid impulse shopping.

Name: SavingStar

Where: www.savingstar.com

Cost: FREE

Available For: iOS and Android

Description: Provides digital coupons for use in a number of grocery stores and drugstores. In addition they are linked to the store's loyalty card. Therefore, when you use the coupons, the rewards are applied to your loyalty card and earn savings and points for you.

At the end of the day, do remember that quality meals are still as important as ever, even if your budget may be reduced.

With healthy meals, you keep your body fit and healthy, thereby decreasing the likelihood of illness and such.

IMPORTANT!

Check out how you can save big on your car, entertainment, grocery, and household expenditures in your exclusive bonus **"Insider Money Saving Tips"** here:

www.RichestManDecoded.com/bonus

#3: Debt Clearance

In a recent analysis by Washington Post, it was reported that student debt is emerging as a public policy issue, especially with young millennials. In fact, 17% of the borrowers are lagging behind in their payments. This represented about at least $1.2 trillion in college loans at the last estimation.

If you are not a student, have you fully paid off your study loan? Or are you still struggling with it?

Debt is a distressing phenomenon, and it overwhelming spreads over many aspects in life such as mortgage loans, car loans and credit card debt etc.

Sounds like a nightmare, yes?

Suffice to say then, debt should be removed and resolved as soon as possible so that there is no overhanging shadow in one's life.
And here is the outline what you should do:

🏛 **Step 1**: Get hold of your credit report. A credit report usually allows financial institutions to decide whether or not to give you credit for a loan, and the interest rate they can charge you. The information in the credit report includes any late payments for loans and the current amount of debt etc.

🏛 **Step 2**: Approach the companies. Based on the credit report, approach the companies that you are indebted to, one at a time. If the amount is small and say, less than $500, it may be feasible to pay it off, provided you have it of course.

It would be best if you could start clearing the debt starting from the largest to the smallest. As you negotiate with the company settlement, do try and persuade them to drop any late charges or miscellaneous charges.

🏛 **Step 3**: Once the company agrees to your proposal for debt settlement, request the agreement in writing. Make sure you obtain all the official receipts etc as you clear the debt.

🏛 **Step 4**: After you've cleared the first company's debt, start on the next. As mentioned earlier, start with the one with the highest amount, unless there is a urgency to other debts.

🏛 **Step 5**: After you clear all your debts, make sure you don't incur any unnecessary ones anymore!

THE LUCKIEST MAN IN BABYLON

At the head of his caravan, proudly rode Sharru Nada, the merchant prince of Babylon. He liked fine cloth and wore rich and becoming robes. He liked fine animals and sat easily upon his spirited Arabian stallion. To look at him one would hardly have guessed his advanced years. Certainly they would not have suspected that he was inwardly troubled.

The journey from Damascus is long and the hardships of the desert many. These he minded not.

The Arab tribes are fierce and eager to loot rich caravans. These he feared not for his many fleet mounted guards were a safe protection.

About the youth at his side, whom he was bringing from Damascus, was he disturbed. This was Hadan Gula, the grandson of his partner of other years, Arad Gula, to whom he felt he owed a debt of gratitude which could never be repaid. He would like to do something for this grandson, but the more he considered this, the more difficult it seemed because of the youth himself.

Eyeing the young man's rings and earrings, he thought to himself, "He thinks jewels are for men, still he has his grandfather's strong face. But his grandfather wore no such gaudy robes. Yet, I sought him to come, hoping I might help him get a start for himself and get away from the wreck his father has made of their inheritance."

Hadan Gula broke in upon his thoughts, "Why dost thou work so hard, riding always with thy caravan upon its long journeys? Dost thou never take time to enjoy life?"

Sharru Nada smiled. "To enjoy life?" he repeated. "What wouldst thou do to enjoy life if thou wert Sharru Nada?"

"If I had wealth equal to thine, I would live like a prince. Never across the hot desert would I ride. I would spend the shekels as fast as they came to my purse. I would wear the richest of robes and the rarest of jewels. That would be a life to my liking, a life worth living." Both men laughed.

"Thy grandfather wore no jewels." Sharru Nada spoke before he thought, then continued jokingly, "Wouldst thou leave no time for work?"

"Work was made for slaves," Hadan Gula responded.

Sharra Nada bit his lip but made no reply, riding in silence until the trail led them to the slope.

Here he reined his mount and pointing to the green valley far away, "See, there is the valley. Look far down and thou canst faintly see the walls of Babylon. The tower is the Temple of Bel. If thine eyes are sharp thou mayest even see the smoke from the eternal fire upon its crest."

"So that is Babylon? Always have I longed to see the wealthiest city in all the world," Hadan Gula commented. "Babylon, where my grandfather started his fortune. Would he were still alive. We would not be so sorely pressed."

"Why wish his spirit to linger on earth beyond its allotted time? Thou and thy father can well carry on his good work."

"Alas, of us, neither has his gift. Father and myself know not his secret for attracting the golden shekels."

Sharru Nada did not reply but gave rein to his mount and rode thoughtfully down the trail to the valley.

Behind them followed the caravan in a cloud of reddish dust. Sometime later they reached the Kings' highway and turned south through the irrigated farms. Three old men plowing a field caught Sharru Nada's attention. They seemed strangely familiar.

How ridiculous! One does not pass a field after forty years and find the same men plowing there. Yet, something within him said they were the same. One, with an uncertain grip, held the plow. The others laboriously plodded beside the oxen, ineffectually beating them with their barrel staves to keep them pulling.

Forty years ago he had envied these men! How gladly he would have exchanged places! But what a difference now. With pride he looked back at his trailing caravan, well- chosen camels and donkeys, loaded high with valuable goods from Damascus. All this was but one of his possessions.

He pointed to the plowers, saying, "Still plowing the same field where they were forty years ago."

"They look it, but why thinkest thou they are the same?"

"I saw them there," Sharru Nada replied. Recollections were racing rapidly through his mind.

Why could he not bury the past and live in the present? Then he saw, as in a picture, the smiling face of Arad Gula. The barrier between himself and the cynical youth beside him dissolved.

But how could he help such a superior youth with his spendthrift ideas and bejeweled hands? Work he could offer in plenty to willing workers, but naught for men who considered themselves too good for work. Yet he owed it to Arad Gula to do something, not a half-hearted attempt. He and Arad Gula had never done things that way. They were not that sort of men.

A plan came almost in a flash. There were objections. He must consider his own family and his own standing. It would be cruel; it would hurt. Being a man of quick decisions, he waived objections and decided to act.

"Wouldst thou be interested in hearing how thy worthy grandfather and myself joined in the partnership which proved so profitable?" he questioned.

"Why not just tell me how thou madest the golden shekels? That is all I need to know," the young man parried.

Sharru Nada ignored the reply and continued, "We start with those men plowing. I was no older than thou. As the column of men in which I marched approached, good old Megiddo, the farmer, scoffed at the slip-shod way in which they plowed. Megiddo was chained next to me. 'Look at the lazy fellows,' he protested, 'the plow holder makes no effort to plow deep, nor do the beaters keep the oxen in the furrow. How can they expect to raise a good crop with poor plowing?'

"Didst thou say Megiddo was chained to thee?" Hadan Gula asked in surprise.

"Yes, with bronze collars about our necks and a length of heavy chain between us. Next to him was Zabado, the sheep thief. I had known him in Harroun. At the end was a man we called Pirate because he told us not his name. We judged him as a sailor as he had entwined serpents tattooed upon his chest in sailor fashion. The column was made up thus so the men could walk in fours."

"Thou wert chained as a slave?" Hadan Gula asked incredulously.

"Did not thy grandfather tell thee I was once a slave?"

"He often spoke of thee but never hinted of this."

"He was a man thou couldst trust with innermost secrets. Thou, too, are a man I may trust, am I not right?" Sharru Nada looked him squarely in the eye.

"Thou mayest rely upon my silence, but I am amazed. Tell me how didst thou come to be a slave?"

Sharru Nada shrugged his shoulders, "Any man may find himself a slave. It was a gaming house and barley beer that brought me disaster. I was the victim of my brother's indiscretions. In a brawl he killed his friend. I was bonded to the widow by my fattier, desperate to keep my brother from being prosecuted under the law. When my father could not raise the silver to free me, she in anger sold me to the slave dealer."

"What a shame and injustice!" Hadan Gula protested. "But tell me, how didst thou regain freedom?"

"We shall come to that, but not yet. Let us continue my tale. As we passed, the plowers jeered at us. One did doff his ragged hat and bow low, calling out, "Welcome to Babylon, guests of the King. He waits for thee on the city walls where the banquet is spread, mud bricks and onion soup.' With that they laughed uproariously.

"Pirate flew into a rage and cursed them roundly. 'What do those men mean by the King awaiting us on the walls?' I asked him.

"To the city walls ye march to carry bricks until the back breaks. Maybe they beat thee to death before it breaks. They won't beat me. Ill kill 'em.'
"Then Megiddo spoke up, 'It doesn't make sense to me to talk of masters beating willing, hard-working slaves to death. Masters like good slaves and treat them well."

"Who wants to work hard?' commented Zabado. 'Those plowers are wise fellows. They're not breaking their backs. Just letting on as if they be.'

"Thou can't get ahead by shirking,' Megiddo protested. If thou plow a hectare, that's a good day's work and any master knows it. But when thou plow only a half, that's shirking. I don't shirk. I like to work and I like to do good work, for work is the best friend I've ever known. It has brought me all the good things I've had, my farm and cows and crops, everything.'

"Yea, and where be these things now?' scoffed Zabado. 'I figure it pays better to be smart and get by without working. You watch Zabado, if we're sold to the walls, he'll be carrying the water bag or some easy job when thou, who like to work, will be breaking thy back carrying bricks.' He laughed his silly laugh.

"Terror gripped me that night. I could not sleep. I crowded close to the guard rope, and when the others slept, I attracted the attention of Godoso who was doing the first guard watch. He was one of those brigand Arabs, the sort of rogue who, if he robbed thee of thy purse, would think he must also cut thy throat.

"Tell me, Godoso,' I whispered, 'when we get to Babylon will we be sold to the walls?'

"Why want to know?' he questioned cautiously.

"Canst thou not understand?' I pleaded. 'I am young. I want to live. I don't want to be worked or beaten to death on the walls. Is there any chance for me to get a good master?'

"He whispered back, 'I tell something. Thou good fellow, give Godoso no trouble. Most times we go first to slave market. Listen now. When buyers come, tell 'em you good worker, like to work hard for good master. Make 'em want to buy. You not make 'em buy, next day you carry brick. Mighty hard work.'

"After he walked away, I lay in the warm sand, looking up at the stars and thinking about work.

What Megiddo had said about it being his best friend made me wonder if it would be my best friend.

Certainly it would be if it helped me out of this.

"When Megiddo awoke, I whispered my good news to him. It was our one ray of hope as we marched toward Babylon. Late in the afternoon we approached the walls and could see the lines of men, like black ants, climbing up and down the steep diagonal paths. As we drew closer, we were amazed at the thousands of men working; some were digging in the moat, others mixed the dirt into mud bricks. The greatest number were carrying the bricks in large baskets up those steep trails to the masons.*

"Overseers cursed the laggards and cracked bullock whips over the backs of those who failed to keep in line. Poor, worn-out fellows were seen to stagger and fall beneath their heavy baskets, unable to rise again. If the lash failed to bring them to their feet, they were pushed to the side of the paths and left writhing in agony.

Soon they would be dragged down to join other craven bodies beside the roadway to await un-sanctified graves. As I beheld the ghastly sight, I shuddered. So this was what awaited my father's son if he failed at the slave market.

*The famous works of ancient Babylon, its walls, temples, hanging gardens and great canals, were built by slave labor, mainly prisoners of war, which explains the inhuman treatment they received.

This force of workmen also included many citizens of Babylon and its provinces who had been sold into slavery because of crimes or financial troubles. It was a common custom for men to put themselves, their wives or their children up as a bond to guarantee payment of loans, legal judgments or other obligations. In case of default, those so bonded were sold into slavery.

"Godoso had been right. We were taken through the gates of the city to the slave prison and next morning marched to the pens in the market.

Here the rest of the men huddled in fear and only the whips of our guard could keep them moving so the buyers could examine them. Megiddo and myself eagerly talked to every man who permitted us to address him.

"The slave dealer brought soldiers from the King's Guard who shackled Pirate and brutally beat him when he protested. As they led him away, I felt sorry for him.

"Megiddo felt that we would soon part. When no buyers were near, he talked to me earnestly to impress upon me how valuable work would be to me in the future: 'Some men hate it. They make it their enemy. Better to treat it like a friend, make thyself like it. Don't mind because it is hard. If thou thinkest about what a good house thou build, then who cares if the beams are heavy and it is far from the well to carry the water for the plaster.

Promise me, boy, if thou get a master, work for him as hard as thou canst. If he does not appreciate all thou do, never mind. Remember, work, well-done, does good to the man who does it. It makes him a better man.' He stopped as a burly farmer came to the enclosure and looked at us critically.

"Megiddo asked about his farm and crops, soon convincing him that he would be a valuable man. After violent bargaining with the slave dealer, the farmer drew a fat purse from beneath his robe, and soon Megiddo had followed his new master out of sight.

"A few other men were sold during the morning. At noon Godoso confided to me that the dealer was disgusted and would not stay over another night but would take all who remained at sundown to the King's buyer. I was becoming desperate when a fat, good-natured man walked up to the wall and inquired if there was a baker among us.

"I approached him saying, "Why should a good baker like thyself seek another baker of inferior ways? Would it not be easier to teach a willing man like myself thy skilled ways? Look at me, I am young, strong and like to work. Give me a chance and I will do my best to earn gold and silver for thy purse."

"He was impressed by my willingness and began bargaining with the dealer who had never noticed me since he had bought me but now waxed eloquent on my abilities, good health and good disposition. I felt like a fat ox being sold to a butcher. At last, much to my joy, the deal was closed. I followed my new master away, thinking I was the luckiest man in Babylon.

"My new home was much to my liking. Nana-naid, my master, taught me how to grind the barley in the stone bowl that stood in the courtyard, how to build the fire in the oven and then how to grind very fine the sesame flour for the honey cakes. I had a couch in the shed where his grain was stored. The old slave housekeeper, Swasti, fed me well and was pleased at the way I helped her with the heavy tasks.

"Here was the chance I had longed for to make myself valuable to my master and, I hoped, to find a way to earn my freedom.

"I asked Nana-naid to show me how to knead the bread and to bake. This he did, much pleased at my willingness. Later, when I could do this well, I asked him to show me how to make the honey cakes, and soon I was doing all the baking. My master was glad to be idle, but Swasti shook her head in disapproval, 'No work to do is bad for any man,' she declared.

"I felt it was time for me to think of a way by which I might start to earn coins to buy my freedom. As the baking was finished at noon, I thought Nana-naid would approve if I found profitable employment for the afternoons and might share my earnings with me. Then the thought came to me, why not bake more of the honey cakes and peddle them to hungry men upon the streets of the city?

"I presented my plan to Nana-naid this way: 'If I can use my afternoons after the baking is finished to earn for thee coins, would it be only fair for thee to share my earnings with me that I might have money of my own to spend for those things which every man desires and needs?

"Fair enough, fair enough,' he admitted. When I told him of my plan to peddle our honey cakes, he was well pleased. 'Here is what we will do,' he suggested. 'Thou sellest them at two for a penny, then half of the pennies will be mine to pay for the flour and the honey and the wood to bake them. Of the rest, I shall take half and thou shall keep half.'

"I was much pleased by his generous offer that I might keep for myself, one-fourth of my sales.

That night I worked late to make a tray upon which to display them. Nana-naid gave me one of his worn robes that I might look well, and Swasti helped me patch it and wash it clean.

"The next day I baked an extra supply of honey cakes. They looked brown and tempting upon the tray as I went along the street, loudly calling my wares. At first no one seemed interested, and I became discouraged. I kept on and later in the afternoon as men became hungry, the cakes began to sell and soon my tray was empty.

"Nana-naid was well pleased with my success and gladly paid me my share. I was delighted to own pennies. Megiddo had been right when he said a master appreciated good work from his slaves.

That night I was so excited over my success I could hardly sleep and tried to figure how much I could earn in a year and how many years would be required to buy my freedom.

"As I went forth with my tray of cakes every day, I soon found regular customers. One of these was none other than thy grandfather, Arad Gula.

He was a rug merchant and sold to the housewives, going from one end of the city the other, accompanied by a donkey loaded high with rugs and a black slave to tend it. He would buy two cakes for himself and two for his slave, always tarrying to talk with me while they ate them.

Thy grandfather said something to me one day that I shall always remember. 'I like thy cakes, boy, but better still I like the fine enterprise with which thou offerest them. Such spirit can carry thee far on the road to success.'

"But how canst thou understand, Hadan Gula, what such words of encouragement could mean to a slave boy, lonesome in a great city, struggling with all he had in him to find a way out of his humiliation?

"As the months went by I continued to add pennies to my purse. It began to have a comforting weight upon my belt. Work was proving to be my best friend Just as Megiddo had said. I was happy but Swasti was worried.

"Thy master, I fear to have him spend so much time at the gaming houses,' she protested.

"I was overjoyed one day to meet my friend Megiddo upon the street. He was leading three donkeys loaded with vegetables to the market. 'I am doing mighty well,' he said.

'My master does appreciate my good work for now I am a foreman. See, he does trust the marketing to me, and also he is sending for my family. Work is helping me to recover from my great trouble. Some day it will help me to buy my freedom and once more own a farm of my own.'

"Time went on and Nana-naid became more and more anxious for me to return from selling. He would be waiting when I returned and would eagerly count and divide our money. He would also urge me to seek further markets and increase my sales.

"Often I went outside the city gates to solicit the overseers of the slaves building the walls. I hated to return to the disagreeable sights but found the overseers liberal buyers. One day I was surprised to see Zabado waiting in line to fill his basket with bricks. He was gaunt and bent, and his back was covered with welts and sores from the whips of the overseers. I was sorry for him and handed him a cake which he crushed into his mouth like a hungry animal. Seeing the greedy look in his eyes, I ran before he could grab my tray.

"Why dost thou work so hard?' Arad Gula said to me one day. Almost the same question thou asked of me today, dost thou remember? I told him what Megiddo had said about work and how it was proving to be my best friend. I showed him with pride my wallet of pennies and explained how I was saving them to buy my freedom.

"When thou art free, what wilt thou do?' he inquired.

"Then,' I answered, I intend to become a merchant.'

"At that, he confided in me. Something I had never suspected. 'Thou knowest not that I, also, am a slave. I am in partnership with my master."

"Stop," demanded Hadan Gula. 'I will not listen to lies defaming my grandfather. He was no slave." His eyes blazed in anger.

Sharru Nada remained calm. "I honor him for rising above his misfortune and becoming a leading citizen of Damascus. Art thou, his grandson, cast of the same mold? Art thou man enough to face true facts, or dost thou prefer to live under false illusions?"

Hadan Gula straightened in his saddle. In a voice suppressed with deep emotion he replied, "My grandfather was beloved by all. Countless were his good deeds.

When the famine came did not his gold buy grain in Egypt and did not his caravan bring it to Damascus and distribute it to the people so none would starve? Now thou sayest he was but a despised slave in Babylon."

"Had he remained a slave in Babylon, then he might well have been despised, but when, through his own efforts, he became a great man in Damascus, the Gods indeed condoned his misfortunes and honored him with their respect,"

Sharru Nada replied.

"After telling me that he was a slave," Sharru Nada continued, 'he explained how anxious he had been to earn his freedom. Now that he had enough money to buy this he was much disturbed as to what he should do. He was no longer making good sales and feared to leave the support of his master.

"I protested his indecision: 'Cling no longer to thy master. Get once again the feeling of being a free man. Act like a free man and succeed like one! Decide what thou desirest to accomplish and then work will aid thee to achieve it!' He went on his way saying he was glad I had shamed him for his cowardice.*

"One day I went outside the gates again, and was surprised to find a great crowd gathering there.

When I asked a man for an explanation he replied: 'Hast thou not heard? An escaped slave who murdered one of the King's guards has been brought to justice and will this day be flogged to death for his crime. Even the King himself is to be here.'

"So dense was the crowd about the flogging post, I feared to go near lest my tray of honey cakes be upset. Therefore, I climbed up the unfinished wall to see over the heads of the people. I was fortunate in having a view of Nebuchadnezzar himself as he rode by in his golden chariot.

Never had I beheld such grandeur, such robes and hangings of gold cloth and velvet.

"I could not see the flogging though I could hear the shrieks of the poor slave. I wandered how one so noble as our handsome King could endure to see such suffering, yet when I saw he was laughing and joking with his nobles, I knew he was cruel and understood why such inhuman tasks were demanded of the slaves building the walls."

"After the slave was dead, his body was hung upon a pole by a rope attached to his leg so all might see. As the crowd began to thin, I went close. On the hairy chest, I saw tattooed, two entwined serpents. It was Pirate. "

"The next time I met Arad Gula he was a changed man. Full of enthusiasm he greeted me: 'Behold, the slave thou knewest is now a free man. There was magic in thy words. Already my sales and my profits are increasing. My wife is overjoyed. She was a free woman, the niece of my master. She much desires that we move to a strange city where no man shall know I was once a slave. Thus our children shall be above reproach for their father's misfortune. Work has become my best helper. It has enabled me to recapture my confidence and my skill to sell."

"I was overjoyed that I had been able even in a small way, to repay him for the encouragement he had given me.

*Slave customs in ancient Babylon, though they may seem inconsistent to us, were strictly regulated by law.

For example, a slave could own property of any kind, even other slaves upon which his master had no claim. Slaves intermarried freely with non-slaves. Children of free mothers were free. Most of the city merchants were slaves. Many of these were in partnership with their masters and wealthy in their own right.

"One evening Swasti came to me in deep distress: 'Thy master is in trouble. I fear for him.

Some months ago he lost much at the gaming tables. He pays not the farmer for his grain nor his honey.

He pays not the money lender. They are angry and threaten him." "Why should we worry over his folly. We are not his keepers,' I replied thoughtlessly.

"Foolish youth, thou understandeth not. To the money lender didst he give thy title to secure a loan. Under the law he can claim thee and sell thee. I know not what to do. He is a good master. Why?

Oh why, should such trouble come upon him?'

"Not were Swasti's fears groundless. While I was doing the baking next morning, the money lender returned with a man he called Sasi. This man looked me over and said I would do.

"The money lender waited not for my master to return but told Swasti to tell him he had taken me. With only the robe on my back and the purse of pennies hanging safely from my belt, I was hurried away from the unfinished baking.

"I was whirled away from my dearest hopes as the hurricane snatches the tree from the forest and casts it into the surging sea. Again a gaming house and barley beer had caused me disaster.

"Sasi was a blunt, gruff man. As he led me across the city, I told him of the good work I had been doing for Nana-naid and said I hoped to do good work for him. His reply offered no encouragement:

"I like not this work. My master likes it not. The King has told him to send me to build a section of the Grand Canal. Master tells Sasi to buy more slaves, work hard and finish quick. Bah, how can any man finish a big job quick?'

"Picture a desert with not a tree, just low shrubs and a sun burning with such fury the water in our barrels became so hot we could scarcely drink it. Then picture rows of men, going down into the deep excavation and lugging heavy baskets of dirt up soft, dusty trails from daylight until dark."

"Picture food served in open troughs from which we helped ourselves like swine. We had no tents, no straw for beds. That was the situation in which I found myself. I buried my wallet in a marked spot, wondering if I would ever dig it up again."

"At first I worked with good will, but as the months dragged on, I felt my spirit breaking. Then the heat fever took hold of my weary body. I lost my appetite and could scarcely eat the mutton and vegetables. At night I would toss in unhappy wakefulness.

"In my misery, I wondered if Zabado had not the best plan, to shirk and keep his back from being broken in work. Then I recalled my last sight of him and knew his plan was not good.

"I thought of Pirate with his bitterness and wondered if it might be just as well to fight and kill. The memory of his bleeding body reminded me that his plan was also useless.

"Then I remembered my last sight of Megiddo. His hands were deeply calloused from hard work but his heart was light and there was happiness on his face. His was the best plan.

"Yet I was just as willing to work as Megiddo; he could not have worked harder than I. Why did not my work bring me happiness and success?

Was it work that brought Megiddo happiness, or was happiness and success merely in the laps of the Gods? Was I to work the rest of my life without gaining my desires, without happiness and success? All of these questions were jumbled in my mind and I had not an answer.

Indeed, I was sorely confused. "Several days later when it seemed that I was at the end of my endurance and my questions still unanswered, Sasi sent for me. A messenger had come from my master to take me back to Babylon. I dug up my precious wallet, wrapped myself in the tattered remnants of my robe and was on my way.

"As we rode, the same thoughts of a hurricane whirling me hither and thither kept racing through my feverish brain. I seemed to be living the weird words of a chant from my native town of Harroun:

Besetting a man like a whirlwind,

Driving him like a storm,

Whose course no one can foliate,

Whose destiny no one can foretell.

"Was I destined to be ever thus punished for I knew not what? What new miseries and disappointments awaited me?

"When we rode to the courtyard of my master's house, imagine my surprise when I saw Arad Gula awaiting me. He helped me down and hugged me like a long lost brother.

"As we went our way I would have followed him as a slave should follow his master, but he would not permit me.

He put his arm about me, saying, 'I hunted everywhere for thee. When I had almost given up hope, I did meet Swasti who told me of the money lender, who directed me to thy noble owner. A hard bargain he did drive and made me pay an outrageous price, but thou art worth it.

Thy philosophy and thy enterprise have been my inspiration to this new success."

"Megiddo's philosophy, not mine,' I interrupted.

"Megiddo's and thine. Thanks to thee both, we are going to Damascus and I need thee for my partner. 'See,' he exclaimed, 'in one moment thou will be a free man!' So saying he drew from beneath his robe the clay tablet carrying my title. This he raised above his head and hurled it to break in a hundred pieces upon the cobble stones. With glee he stamped upon the fragments until they were but dust.

"Tears of gratitude filled my eyes. I knew I was the luckiest man in Babylon. "Work, thou see, by this, in the time of my greatest distress, didst prove to be my best friend.

My willingness to work enabled me to escape from being sold to join the slave gangs upon the walls. It also so impressed thy grandfather, he selected me for his partner."

Then Hadan Gula questioned, "Was work my grandfather's secret key to the golden shekels?"

"It was the only key he had when I first knew him," Sharru Nada replied. "Thy grandfather enjoyed working. The Gods appreciated his efforts and rewarded him liberally."

"I begin to see," Hadan Gula was speaking thoughtfully. "Work attracted his many friends who admired his industry and the success it brought.

Work brought him the honors he enjoyed so much in Damascus. Work brought him all those things I have approved. And I thought work was fit only for slaves."

"Life is rich with many pleasures for men to enjoy," Sharru Nada commented.

"Each has its place. I am glad that work is not reserved for slaves. Were that the case I would be deprived of my greatest pleasure. Many things do I enjoy but nothing takes the place of work."

Sharru Nada and Hadan Gula rode in the shadows of the towering walls up to the massive, bronze gates of Babylon.

At their approach the gate guards jumped to attention and respectfully saluted an honored citizen. With head held high Sharru Nada led the long caravan through the gates and up the streets of the city.

"I have always hoped to be a man like my grandfather," Hadan Gula confided to him. "Never before did I realize just what kind of man he was. This thou hast shown me. Now that I understand, I do admire him all the more and feel more determined to be like him. I fear I can never repay thee for giving me the true key to his success.

From this day forth, I shall use his key. I shall start humbly as he started, which befits my true station far better than jewels and fine robes."

So saying Hadan Gula pulled the jeweled baubles from his ears and the rings from his fingers. Then reining his horse, He dropped back and rode with deep respect behind the Leader of the caravan.

SUMMARY
Guide

Sharru Nada, a wealthy merchant, was on his way back to city of Babylon. With him was Hadan Gula, the grandson of his business partner Arad Gula.

Hadan Gula was lazy and materialistic, and did not look to hard work. This was evident when he asked Sharru Nada why did he not enjoy himself if he had such riches? Why did he have to take a long journey from Damascus back to Babylon?

As they reached Babylon, Hadan Gula was eager to see the city, because this was where his grandfather started his fortune. In fact he wanted to know how his grandfather started his fortune.

To that, Sharru Nada instead narrated his tale:

He was a slave and was bound to Babylon to be sold, together with Megiddo the farmer, Zabado the sheep thief and Pirate the tattooed sailor. As they passed some plowing farmers, Megiddo remarked on their lazy ways. Zabado retorted that they were wise not to break their backs.

That night, Sharru Nada was unable to sleep because he was worried about his fate and fearful that he would be sold to carry bricks for the rest of his life. Godoso the night watch guard advised him something surprising - At the slave market, he was to actively promote himself so that he would be bought by a good master.

At the slave market, Megiddo managed to convince a man of his worth, because he was knowledgeable about farming and crops, and he was swiftly bought. Sharru Nada saw his chance when a man Nana-naid was enquiring whether there was a baker amongst them. Though he had no experience, Sharru Nada presented himself as strong, hardworking and willing to learn, and he was thus bought too.

Nana-naid taught Sharru Nada many tasks and he quickly mastered them. The latter also assisted the slave housekeeper Swasti with her heavy tasks.

Nana-naid soon taught Sharru Nada baking, and an idea came to him: Since his baking duties ended at noon, what if he could bake some more and peddle them to the hungry men of the streets? (He was also secretly thinking of buying his own freedom if he could come up with his sum of money).

Nana-naid was impressed by his idea and agreed to his plan, even allowing Sharru Nada to take a cut out of the earnings.

One day, Sharru Nada met Arad Gula a rug merchant who was impressed with his entrepreneurship while on his rounds to sell the cakes. When he learned that Sharru Nada wanted to buy his own freedom and become a merchant, Arad Gula then revealed that he was also a slave, but in partnership with his master.

During an occasion where he was peddling outside, Sharru Nada was shocked to find Pirate being hanged for escaping from the King's service. Earlier he had bumped into Zabado who was in a sorry state: gaunt and bent from carrying bricks. And he wondered about his eventual fate.

Sharru Nada met Arad Gula again who was contemplating moving away - his wife, the niece of Arad Gula's master, wanted them to move to a new city so that their children would grow up not knowing that their father was once a slave.

One day, Sasi the moneylender came and took Sharru Nada away to join the others in building the Grand Canal, because Nana-naid was in his debt and could not pay.

When Sharru Nada thought he was unable to bear the work anymore, he was summoned back to Babylon. To his surprise Arad Gula bought him from Sasi, because he wanted Sharru Nada to work along with him.

At the end of this story, Hadan Gula finally understood how he was the luckiest man of Babylon, and how his grandfather, and Sharru Nada, came to be so successful - because of hard work.

LEARNING/LESSON

One of the richest men in the world, Hong Kong's Li Ka-shing had a very humble beginning: He started working as a teenager in a plastics factory when he was just 15 years of age. By 19 he was the factory general manager.

By the age of 22, in 1950, he started his own business, and the rest is history. Li Ka-shing is now worth US $3.3 billion in 2015.Indeed, while some people do make it due to luck, it is undeniable that hard work and effort are the fundamental requisites for success. Sometimes though when the going gets tough, how do you get the motivation to keep on going?

Here are 4 strategies you may want to consider:

🏛 **The End Goal** - Be very clear about your end goal. Remember the vision board in the chapter "The Richest Man In Babylon"? Keep that vision board firmly in your mind. Use that to motivate yourself, because you do want that don't you? That wealth, that success?

🏛 **The Physical Health** - Many times people may find it difficult to be motivated, not because they don't have a clear goal, or don't feel inspired , but because they are physically exhausted. Do you feel tired all the time? Are you sleepy all the time? Do you eat well or binge on junk food 24/7? It is important that you get the minimal number of hours of sleep (7 hours), eat well and live well with positive thoughts and cheerful disposition. A measure of constructive stress is necessary because you are working your way to be a successful and wealthy person!

🏛 **The Habits** - When an action becomes a habit, it is so much easier to do it, instead of forcing the self to do it. Start with small, productive habits with reference to your end goal. Take action on small task to lead up to bigger things, and track your own progress and evaluation.

🏛 **The Reward** - The reward is one of the most easiest ways to get moving. The road to the end-goal could be all sweat and hard work, and it may not get easier. Dangle a treat for yourself. This both gives you a pat on your back for the effort you put in, and also makes you look forward to the end-goal culmination!

CONCLUSION

As mentioned at the start of this book, I decided to publish The Richest Man In Babylon Decoded because I wanted to share the wisdoms that have benefited me immensely in my own journey toward success. If you've read George Clason's original text, you may have some difficulty understanding some of the archaic language used.

However, because I believe in the wisdoms within its pages, the very same wisdoms that have helped me overcome so much in my life, I felt the need to distill the knowledge that Clason imparted in his original text into a much more accessible form, something that even the common man on the streets can understand.

Which is why I hope that the Chapter Summaries and Learning Lessons have made it easier for you to understand the wisdoms in Clason's original text.

So what have we learned?

We have learned the importance of having the right mindset before embarking on any journey for wealth. We must set our mind toward wealth if we are to welcome wealth into our lives. Visualization helps us attune our mind and steer it toward manifesting wealth.

We have also learned the importance of paying one's self first. Save 10% of whatever you earn in a bank account separate from the one that you use for expenditure.

Let your money work for you. If you choose to invest, be wise in your investments. Do not blindly heed the advice of those who claim to know better. Do as much homework as you can before you make any investment decision.

Re-invest the returns of your investment. Always keep in mind the bigger picture; your investments are meant to secure your future. Do not be short-sighted and spend the returns frivolously on non-essential wants.

Spend less than what you earn, and apply smart spending strategies for the money that you do spend.

Curb impulse spending. When you see something you want to purchase, take a breath and wait for a certain period of time before you proceed with the purchase. If you still feel strongly about it by the end of the time-out period, only then can you purchase the item (if you have the funds or budget to do so).

Be aware of your spending pattern. Change it when you find yourself spending excessively. Don't be fooled by sales that tempt you with perceived savings. Ask yourself if you REALLY need the item on sale.

Where your home is concerned, it may be better to buy than to rent.

Put in place strategies that will provide you and your loved ones with future income, so that you or your loved ones are cared for in the event of retirement or death.

Never stop learning. Always keep your brain active through constant learning. Keeping yourself educated throughout your life will ensure that you won't miss out on any wealth building opportunities that may present themselves to you.

Make your own luck. Keep your mind open for opportunities that may be potentially rewarding. As long as you stay positive and committed toward achieving your goal, you will create your own good luck.

Be prudent when lending money, especially to ones close to you. When money comes between you and a loved one, it may be hard to resolve issues without feelings being hurt.
Get some form of insurance. Insurance is a great and inexpensive way to obtain security for the future. Be it health insurance, auto insurance, or even disability insurance, one must always be prepared for unforeseen circumstances.

Don't be frivolous with credit cards. The convenience of credit cards makes it easy for most people to abuse them, and forget that they're essentially owing the banks. The more credit cards you have, the more you can, and WILL charge.

It's amazing how so much of these ancient wisdoms apply to our modern day life. I hope that the learning lessons presented in this book have helped you understand the key principles to obtaining wealth, and that you are able to use at least some of the practical strategies put forth in these pages to help you attain the kind of wealth that you've been looking for.

To your abundant wealth,

Winter Vee

Winter Vee

MY SPECIAL GIFT TO YOU...

Congratulations on having taken the first step toward abundance and prosperity! As a special "thank you" for picking up Richest Man In Babylon Decoded, I'd like to offer you 2 special bonuses that will really help you take advantage of the lessons you're about to learn in this book.

1. Affirmations for Affluence

A companion to the chapter "Seven Cures For A Lean Purse," these affirmations will embed powerful new beliefs and behaviors into your subconscious, and help you attain a mind focused on limitless opportunities for wealth. This is the secret to getting the kind of abundant life that you deserve.

2. Insider Money Saving Tips

These invaluable tips will help you save thousands of dollars a year on necessities if done right. You're getting advice straight from today's best financial experts, at absolutely no cost at all. Save big on your car, entertainment, grocery, and home maintenance, so you can look forward to a fatter bank account for your retirement needs, or even if you need a little extra cash to treat yourself every year with a well deserved holiday.

To your abundant wealth,

Winter Vee

Winter Vee

CLAIM YOUR BONUSES WORTH $197 HERE:

www.RichestManDecoded.com/bonus